POSSESSING THE PROMISE OF GOD

A Study of Joshua & Judges

Jack W. Hayford
with
Mark Wilson

THOMAS NELSON PUBLISHERS
Nashville

Possessing the Promise of God
A Study of Joshua & Judges
Copyright © 1997 by Jack W. Hayford

Published in Nashville, Tennessee, by Thomas Nelson, Inc.

Printed in the United States of America
1 2 3 4 5 6 7 8 — 01 00 99 98

CONTENTS

Possessing the Promise of God (A Study of Joshua & Judges) is one of a series of study guides that focus exciting, discovery-geared coverage of Bible book and power themes—all prompting toward dynamic, Holy Spirit-filled living.

About the Executive Editor

JACK W. HAYFORD, noted pastor, teacher, writer, and composer, is the Executive Editor of the complete series, working with the publisher in the conceiving and developing of each of the books.

Dr. Hayford is Senior Pastor of The Church On The Way, the First Foursquare Church of Van Nuys, California. He and his wife, Anna, have four married children, all of whom are active in either pastoral ministry or vital church life. As General Editor of the *Spirit-Filled Life*® *Bible,* Pastor Hayford led a four-year project, which has resulted in the availability of one of today's most practical and popular study Bibles. He is author of more than twenty books, including *A Passion for Fullness, The Beauty of Spiritual Language, Rebuilding the Real You,* and *Prayer Is Invading the Impossible.* His musical compositions number over four hundred songs, including the widely sung "Majesty."

About the Writer

MARK WILSON is associate professor of New Testament in the undergraduate School of Theology at Oral Roberts University in Tulsa, Oklahoma. Previously he served as general editor of the Christian Broadcasting Network's *Living By The Book* discipleship curriculum. He was also co-coordinator of the Praying Through the Window II global prayer movement in 1995, editing its official guide *Praying Through the 100 Gateway Cities.* He is the editor of and a contributor in *Spirit and Renewal: Essays in Honor of J. Rodman Williams* and has revised and updated four volumes by the British scholar William M. Ramsay.

Dr. Wilson is married to Dindy Wilson and has four grown children, Leelannee, Winema, James, and David. He has earned degrees from Christ for the Nations Institute, Dallas, Tex.; Trinity Bible College, Ellendale, N.D.; and Regent University, Virginia Beach, Va. He was recently awarded the degree of Doctor of Literature and Philosophy in Biblical Studies from the University of South Africa, Pretoria, South Africa.

THE GIFT
THAT KEEPS ON GIVING

One of the most precious gifts God has given us is His Word, the Bible. Wrapped in the glory and sacrifice of His Son and delivered by the power and ministry of His Spirit, it is a treasured gift—the gift that keeps on giving, because the Giver it reveals is inexhaustible in His love and grace.

Tragically, though, fewer and fewer people are opening this gift and seeking to understand what it's all about and how to use it. They often feel intimidated by it. It requires some assembly, and its instructions are hard to comprehend sometimes. How does the Bible fit together anyway? What does this ancient Book have to say to us who are looking toward the twenty-first century? Will taking the time and energy to understand its instructions and to fit it all together really help you and me?

Yes. Yes. Without a shred of doubt.

The *Spirit-Filled Life® Bible Discovery Guide* series is designed to help you unwrap, assemble, and enjoy all God has for you in the pages of Scripture. It will focus your time and energy on the books of the Bible, the people and places they describe, and the themes and life applications that flow thick from its pages like honey oozing from a beehive.

So you can get the most out of God's Word, this series has a number of helpful features:

 WORD WEALTH

"WORD WEALTH" provides definitions of key terms.

 BEHIND THE SCENES

"BEHIND THE SCENES" supplies information about cultural practices, doctrinal disputes, business trades, etc.

 AT A GLANCE

"AT A GLANCE" features helpful maps and charts.

BIBLE EXTRA

"BIBLE EXTRA" will guide you to other resources that will enable you to glean more from the Bible's wealth.

PROBING THE DEPTHS

"PROBING THE DEPTHS," will explain controversial issues raised by particular lessons and cite Bible passages and other sources to help you come to your own conclusions.

FAITH ALIVE

The "FAITH ALIVE" feature will help you see and apply the Bible to your day-to-day needs.

The only resources you need to complete and apply these study guides are a heart and mind open to the Holy Spirit, a prayerful attitude, and a pencil and a Bible. Of course, you may draw upon other sources, but these study guides are comprehensive enough to give you all you need to gain a good, basic understanding of the Bible book being covered and how you can apply its themes and counsel to your life.

A word of warning, though. By itself, Bible study will not transform your life. It will not give you power, peace, joy, comfort, hope, and a number of other gifts God longs for you to unwrap and enjoy. Through Bible study, you will grow in your understanding of the Lord, His kingdom and your place in it, but you must be sure to rely on the Holy Spirit to guide your study and your application of the Bible's truths. He, Jesus promised, was sent to teach us "all things" (John 14:26; cf. 1 Cor. 2:13). Bathe your study time in prayer, asking the Spirit of God to illuminate the text, enlighten your mind, humble your will, and comfort your heart. He will never let you down.

My prayer and goal for you is that as you unwrap and begin to explore God's Book for living His way, the Holy Spirit will fill every fiber of your being with the joy and power God longs to give all His children. So read on. Be diligent. Stay open and submissive to Him. You will not be disappointed. He promises you!

Lesson 1/*Preparing for Possession*
Joshua 1:1—2:24

Only a narrow channel of water separated free Britain from occupied France in the spring of 1944. For the Allied forces to defeat the Nazis and liberate Europe, this 60–100 mile expanse had to be crossed. For two years men and materials had been gathered in England in preparation for the strike. Gen. Dwight D. Eisenhower was responsible for what British prime minister Winston Churchill called "the most difficult and complicated operation ever to take place." Planning, training, and timing were the keys.

Finally, Eisenhower gave the order to invade Normandy, and at midnight on June 6, 1944, the longest day began. During the next night and day 175,000 soldiers with their equipment, including 50,000 vehicles such as motorcycles, tanks, and armored bulldozers, were transported across the English Channel. They were carried or supported by 5,333 ships and boats and almost 11,000 airplanes. Although victory on the beaches at Utah, Omaha, and Juno was not instantaneous, D-day turned the tide of World War II and changed the course of history.[1]

In *Possessing the Promise of God* we will follow the children of Israel, who themselves are facing the battle of their lives. In the Book of Joshua we first see the Israelites standing on the bank of the Jordan River before finally taking possession of the Promised Land. Then in the Book of Judges the Israelites encounter the challenges of living in the Promised Land. Throughout our study we will examine the biblical conditions required by God for possessing His promises.

We begin in the Book of Joshua, whose theme is "Taking

the Promise of God." The Book of Joshua shows how God led
His people step-by-step to possess the land He had promised
them. Here we will learn the spiritual principles that allowed the
Israelites to defeat their enemies. These same principles will
assist you in gaining God's promises for your own Christian life.
Our battles today as Christians are not on a literal battlefield
against human enemies. Instead they are of a spiritual nature,
but just as real—sickness, financial crisis, marital strife, family
problems. We know that God promises victory in these day-to-
day struggles, but often that victory seems just out of reach.
The Israelites were likewise promised a land flowing with milk
and honey. But that land was inhabited by giants who seemed
invincible. Yet as they were faithful and obedient to God, each
giant was overcome. Get ready to overcome the giants and possess your land!

INTRODUCTION

The Book of Joshua follows the first five books of Moses
called the Pentateuch, or the Law. In the Hebrew Bible Joshua
begins a new section called the Prophets. It further falls into a
subsection called the Former Prophets consisting of Joshua,
Judges, Samuel, and Kings. In the English Bible, whose order
follows the Greek Old Testament, these books (with Samuel
and Kings now divided) begin a section of twelve historical
books. These twelve books chronicle the 950-year history of
Israel and Judah from the possession of the Promised Land to
the restoration following the Exile.

The Jewish writing called the Talmud identifies Joshua as
the author of the book. Joshua 24:26 states that Joshua wrote
his words before the people in the Book of the Law, so he was
responsible for at least some of Joshua's contents. Yet another
author was also clearly involved, for Joshua's death is recorded
in the final chapter (24:29–32). Other passages were likewise
written after his death: Caleb's conquest of Hebron (14:6–15),
Othniel's victory (15:13–17), and the Danite migration (19:47).
The use of the phrase "to this day," which recurs ten times, suggests that a period of time had elapsed between the events
described and the composition of the book. And the use of the

pronouns "we" (5:1) and "us" (5:6) likewise suggests that the author was an eyewitness to some of the events.[2]

AT A GLANCE[3]

FOCUS	CONQUEST OF CANAAN		SETTLEMENT IN CANAAN				
REFERENCE	1:1 _____	6:1 _____	13:8 _____	14:1 _____	20:1 _____	22:1 _____	24:33
DIVISION	PREPARATION OF ISRAEL	CONQUEST OF CANAAN	SETTLEMENT OF EAST JORDAN	SETTLEMENT OF WEST JORDAN	SETTLEMENT RELIGIOUS COMMUNITY	CONDITIONS FOR CONTINUED SETTLEMENT	
TOPIC	ENTERING CANAAN	CONQUERING CANAAN	DIVIDING CANAAN				
	PREPARATION	SUBJECTION	POSSESSION				
LOCATION	JORDAN RIVER	CANAAN	TWO AND A HALF TRIBES—EAST JORDAN NINE AND A HALF TRIBES—WEST JORDAN				
TIME	c. 1 MONTH	c. 7 YEARS	c. 8 YEARS				

Nelson's Complete Book of Bible Maps and Charts © 1993 by Thomas Nelson, Inc.

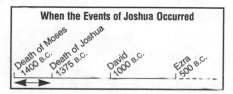

When the Events of Joshua Occurred

Death of Moses 1400 B.C. Death of Joshua 1375 B.C. David 1000 B.C. Ezra 500 B.C.

BEHIND THE SCENES

Who is this remarkable man Joshua, the hero of our story? Joshua first appears in Scripture in Exodus 24:13, where he accompanies Moses to the top of Mount Sinai for a forty-day visitation with God. He is the son of Nun and grandson of Elishama, a chief of the tribe of Ephraim (1 Chron. 7:27; Num. 1:10). Although he is not a Levite, Joshua is appointed by Moses to serve in the tabernacle. There he would remain for days to fellowship with the Lord when Moses returns to the camp. Joshua led the repulsion of an Amalekite attack at

Rephidim (Ex. 17:9). He later served as Ephraim's representative when Moses sent twelve spies to check out the land of Canaan (Num. 13:8). Only he and Caleb brought back a good report, and for their faithfulness these two men are permitted to enter this land of milk and honey (Num. 14:30). Before his death Moses passes on the mantle of leadership to his assistant Joshua, who is filled with the spirit of wisdom (Deut. 34:9).[4]

What was the significance of Moses' act of laying his hands on Joshua? (Num. 27:18–23)

GOD'S CHARGE TO JOSHUA (JOSH. 1:1–9)

The Book of Joshua opens with the nation of Israel ready to possess the Promised Land. Because of unbelief and disobedience, the generation that left Egypt in the Exodus has died after forty years of wandering in the wilderness. Their children are now poised on the east bank of the Jordan River. Before the Israelites can receive their possession, God confirms Joshua's leadership by exhorting him to complete the task begun by Moses. He assures Joshua that He will be with him as He was with Moses. And He promises that every place where the soles of their feet will tread is to be their possession. For the struggle ahead Joshua is repeatedly charged by God to be strong and courageous.

What territory was promised to Israel as its possession? (Josh. 1:4)

How could Israel ensure that it would be prosperous and enjoy good success in the Promised Land? (Josh. 1:7)

Upon what were the Israelites to meditate day and night, so that it would not depart from their mouths? (Josh. 1:8)

BEHIND THE SCENES

The Book of Deuteronomy concludes with Moses dying at the age of 120 in Moab, east of the Dead Sea. Neither his eyesight nor his natural strength were diminished in his old age (Deut. 34:7). Only one incident marred the life of this unique servant of God, "whom the LORD knew face to face" (Deut. 34:10). Because Moses disobeyed at the water of Meribah by striking the rock instead of speaking to it, God forbade him to enter the Promised Land (Num. 20:7–13). However, before his death he is allowed to view it from Mount Nebo. Perhaps it was Joshua who buried Moses near Beth Peor and purposely concealed the burial site so it would not become a shrine for the idolatry-prone Israelites (Deut. 34:1–6).

WORD WEALTH

The name **Joshua** in Hebrew is *Yehoshua,* meaning "the LORD is salvation."[5] Its simplified form *Yeshua* is found later in Nehemiah 8:17. The Greek translation of the Old Testament, produced around 300 B.C., translates Joshua's name here as *Iesous,* which likewise means "the LORD is salvation." This is the same Greek name given to Jesus throughout the Greek New Testament. The writer of Hebrews uses *Iesous* to speak both of Joshua and Jesus. That their names are identical suggests that Joshua is an Old Testament type of Jesus. Even as Joshua led the Israelites into the physical Promised Land, Jesus now leads the church—the new people of God—into the promises of the new covenant. And like the sinless Jesus, Joshua is the only Old Testament hero whose character is blameless. This relationship is why the Book of Joshua is so important to believers today.

FAITH ALIVE

In Joshua 1:5 God gives Joshua the wonderful promise, "I will not leave you nor forsake you." Moses earlier gave this promise to the people of Israel (Deut. 31:6) and to Joshua (Deut. 31:8). The writer of Hebrews likewise quotes this promise (Heb. 13:5) to reassure his readers of God's commitment to provide for their material needs.

Do you feel God has ever abandoned or forsaken you at some time or in a certain area of your life?

If so, how does God's promise relate to your particular need in that area?

 ## WORD WEALTH

Be strong (Heb. *chazaq*) also means to be of good courage, be established, behave self-valiantly.[6] God's charge to Joshua to be strong and of good courage is repeated three times in the opening chapter (Josh. 1:6, 7, 9). The people likewise answer Joshua with the same word of exhortation in Joshua 1:18. This command reiterates a similar one given at the close of Deuteronomy by Moses to the Israelites (Deut. 31:7) and by God to Joshua (Deut. 31:23) at his commissioning to leadership.

Why do you think Joshua is repeatedly admonished to be strong and of good courage?

In the transition of leadership from Moses to Joshua, why was it important for the Israelites to know that their new leader was strong and courageous?

 ## FAITH ALIVE

Strength and courage are two virtues necessary for receiving God's promises.

What promise has God recently made to you?

In what way do you particularly need strength and courage to receive that promise?

 ## Bible Extra

Certain key terms are emphasized repeatedly in chapter 1. Find the verses where these terms are found:

• Moses

• Give

• Land

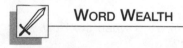 ## Word Wealth

The Hebrew word *hagah,* translated "meditate," likewise means "growl," "mutter," or "groan." In the ancient world meditation was not done silently, but involved speaking with oneself in a low mutter.[7] This same practice can still be seen in Jerusalem today as the Orthodox Jews meditate on, or mutter, the law of God as they stand before the Western Wall.

God tells Joshua that his success in leading Israel into the Promised Land will depend on whether he continually meditates on the Book of the Law (Josh. 1:8). The psalmist likewise states that the blessed are those who meditate on God's law day and night (Ps. 1:2). God's mighty works and majesty are also worthy of meditation (Ps. 143:5; 145:5). Meditation begins in the heart, the center of our emotional and rational life. Hence David cries out that the meditation of his heart be acceptable in God's sight (Ps. 19:14).

In the New Testament the practice is reiterated by Paul when he writes Timothy to meditate on his instructions (1 Tim. 4:15). Paul likewise suggests a number of good things that the Philippians should meditate on (Phil. 4:8). Scripture enjoins all Christians to meditate regularly, and the practice is not reserved just for those on a retreat or apart in a monastery.

FAITH ALIVE

The condition for receiving the promise of prosperity and success is that we meditate on continually and observe faithfully God's commandments in the Scriptures.

When do you spend time reading the Bible each day? If you don't, how can you rearrange your priorities so that time is made?

What are some ways that you meditate on God's Word?

How do you obey in practical ways when the Holy Spirit speaks to you from the Scriptures?

PRESERVING UNITY (JOSH. 1:10–18)

Before Joshua can launch the invasion, he must first resolve a potential problem. The tribes of Reuben and Gad along with the half-tribe of Manasseh have already received their promised inheritance on the east bank of the Jordan River (Deut. 3:12–17). If these tribes fail to cross over and fight with the rest, Israel's unified effort to take the Promised Land will be jeopardized. Therefore Joshua reminds these tribes of Moses' command that they cannot enjoy their inheritance until their fellow Israelites possess the land beyond the Jordan (Deut. 3:18–20). However, the women, children, and livestock of these tribes are allowed to stay behind.

Do you think that the tribes of Reuben, Gad, and Manasseh were eager to fight now that they had their own land?

When could these tribes return to their own land? (Josh. 1:15)

What was the punishment for those who refused to cross over and fight? (Josh. 1:18)

 ## FAITH ALIVE

Unity is important for any spiritual venture to succeed. David likens the blessing of unity to oil running down the high priest's beard or dew descending on Mount Hermon (Ps. 133:2, 3). Without unity it is difficult for God's kingdom purposes to be fulfilled.

Are you a person who encourages unity or sows division in your church?

In what situation in your home or community might you encourage unity and reconciliation?

THE FAITH OF A HARLOT (JOSH. 2:1–24)

Two spies are sent from the camp at Acacia Grove to reconnoiter the enemy's position across the river at Jericho. There the spies lodge with a harlot named Rahab, who saves their lives when the king of Jericho tries to arrest them. For her role in their rescue, the spies promise Rahab that she and her family will be saved when the city is destroyed. The only requirement is that she hang a scarlet cord from her window. The spies safely escape from the city and the king's pursuers. Their positive report back at the camp signals that the period of preparation is over and the time to possess the land has come.

Was Rahab justified in telling a lie to the king to protect the spies? (Josh. 2:6)

What had Rahab heard that caused her to believe in God? (Josh. 2:9–11)

What condition did the spies place upon Rahab for the rescue of her and her family? (Josh. 2:18–19)

 BIBLE EXTRA

Acacia Grove (Heb. *Shittim*) was an important site in Israel's history. Situated in the Plains of Moab, northeast of the Dead Sea, it apparently got its name from the abundance of thorny acacia trees in the area. Acacia wood was used to build the ark of the covenant and parts of the tabernacle (Ex. 25:10, 23, 28; 26:15). At Acacia Grove Moabite women seduced the Israelite men into idolatry, causing God to send a plague that killed 24,000 Israelites (Num. 25:1–3). Moses took a census here for the purpose of military conscription (Num. 26:2). It was Israel's final camping site before crossing into Canaan (Num. 33:49).[8]

 BEHIND THE SCENES

The two spies did not go to Rahab's house to indulge in sinful activity but to find lodging. In the ancient world public inns had a reputation as houses of ill repute. Therefore God-fearing strangers to a city would wait at the gate or in the square for residents to offer hospitality in their home (see Gen. 19:1–3). But the spies were not looking for hospitality, but rather for information. The public inn would have the most traffic and draw the least attention to them. However, the king was monitoring all foreigners in the city because of the nearby Israelite threat, and the spies were spotted.

FAITH ALIVE

Rahab's lifestyle hardly qualifies her as a model of virtue. That God would use someone like her shows He is truly no respecter of persons and that He was looking at the faith in her heart.

Have you ever wondered whether God can use you in ministry because of a skeleton in the closet from your life before Christ?

Like Rahab, whom have you helped in need recently?

BIBLE EXTRA

Rahab is mentioned three times in the New Testament. In Matthew 1:5 she is named in the genealogy of Jesus Christ. Her husband was Salmon and their son was Boaz, who later married Ruth. Like the other women mentioned in this genealogy, Rahab has sexual impropriety as part of her past. Matthew seeks to counteract the scandal of Jesus' out-of-wedlock conception by Mary and of his doubtful paternity by Joseph. His genealogy demonstrates how God uses people whose reputations are less than perfect to advance His kingdom purposes.

The writer of Hebrews includes Rahab among those in his lineup of faith (Heb. 11:31). Her faith in God was demonstrated by her reception of the spies, who later saved her life when Jericho fell. Finally, James cites Rahab, along with Abraham, as examples of those who were justified because of their works (James 2:25). Rahab's "work" was to save the lives of the spies who came to Jericho. This harlot, converted to the God of Israel, serves as an important Old Testament example of faith and action.

FAITH ALIVE

How have you demonstrated your faith through action(s) recently?

List some other "works" through which you might show your faith.

BIBLE EXTRA

The early church fathers viewed the scarlet cord as a type of the atonement. As long as Rahab displayed the cord, she and her family were saved. A redemptive sacrifice had earlier saved the Israelites in Egypt. When they placed the blood of a lamb over the doorposts of their houses (Ex. 12:21–23), the Angel of Death passed over them. Christians are likewise saved by the blood of the Lamb, Jesus Christ (John 1:29; Rev. 5:6), because without the shedding of His blood there is no remission of sins (Heb. 9:22).

What does the scarlet cord in the window symbolize to you? (Josh. 2:18, 21)

FAITH ALIVE

Like Rahab, are you exercising your faith to secure the salvation of your family members?

Which relatives are you believing will come under the protection of the scarlet cord representing the blood of Jesus Christ?

1. Stephen E. Ambrose, *D-Day June 6, 1944: The Climactic Battle of World War II* (New York: Simon & Schuster, 1994), 24–25.

2. *Spirit-Filled Life® Bible* (Nashville: Thomas Nelson Publishers, 1991), 304, "Author."

3. *Nelson's Complete Book of Bible Maps & Charts* (Nashville: Thomas Nelson Publishers, 1996), 67, "Joshua at a Glance," "When the Events in Joshua Occurred."

4. *Nelson's New Illustrated Bible Dictionary* (Nashville: Thomas Nelson Publishers, 1995), 705–6, "Joshua."

5. Ibid., 705.

6. James Strong, *New Strong's Exhaustive Concordance* (Nashville: Thomas Nelson, 1995), "Dictionary of the Hebrew Bible" #2388.

7. *International Standard Bible Encyclopedia*, Vol. 3 (Grand Rapids: Eerdmans, 1986), 305–6, "Meditation."

8. *Nelson's New Illustrated Bible Dictionary*, 3–4, "Abel Acacia Grove."

Lesson 2/Entering God's Promise
Joshua 3:1—6:27

Grand Forks, North Dakota, knows about floods. In the spring of 1997 the Red River between North Dakota and Minnesota crested at a height that occurs only once in 500 years. Despite dikes and sandbags, the swollen river spilled into town after town along its flood plain. In its wake the flood left damages running in the billions of dollars. The city of Grand Forks was hit hardest. Its 40,000 residents were forced to evacuate their homes and live for weeks at nearby emergency shelters. For many the material possessions could be easily replaced; it was the personal items—the photo albums, the family heirlooms—that were the hardest to lose.

In the midst of such suffering came a promise. An anonymous female donor living in California, later identified as Mrs. Ray Kroc, wife of the late founder of McDonalds, approached Grand Forks officials. She offered to give each resident whose home was damaged a check for $2,000. Although this offer provided only minimal compensation for those who had lost everything, it brought hope and the realization that someone saw their need and cared enough to do something about it.

Before the Israelites could receive their promise from God, they likewise had to contend with a flooded river. As they stood on the Jordan's swollen banks, they surely must have wondered how they would get to the other side. And once across, there were still those walled cities inhabited by the "giants" seen by the twelve spies. This lesson gives the dramatic account of how Israel crossed over to the Promised Land.

CROSSING INTO THE PROMISED LAND (JOSH. 3:1–17)

The ark of the covenant symbolized God's presence with His people. During their earlier journeys in the wilderness, the Israelites were led by the cloud that hovered over the ark (Num. 10:33–36). God's presence had been so important to Moses that he had vowed not to go forward unless God led the nation (Ex. 33:14–17). Now the Israelites stand poised to enter the Promised Land, again needing God's leading presence. They can be assured that God will be with them because they are at this point by His assignment, not by their own choice. And they can be assured also by His word through the two spies: "Truly the LORD has delivered all the land into our hands" (Josh. 2:24).

BEHIND THE SCENES

The ark of the covenant was built at Sinai according to the pattern revealed by God (Ex. 25:10–21; 37:1–9). From above the mercy seat, God promised to meet with Moses and to give him the commandments for Israel (Ex. 25:22; Num. 7:89). Only the family of Kohath among the Levites was allowed to care for the ark (Num. 3:30–31). Whenever the camp of Israel moved during the forty years, the ark went before it accompanied by the divine cloud (Num. 10:33–34). Before his death Moses wrote a book containing God's commandments and instructed the Levites to put it beside the ark as a witness against Israel (Deut. 31:24–26).

As Israel prepared to cross over, Joshua ordered that the travel protocol initiated by Moses was likewise to be followed in the Promised Land: the Kohathites were to go first, carrying the ark into the Jordan; then the people were to follow. The ark later plays a key role in the destruction of Jericho (Josh. 6:7–16) and in the renewal of the covenant at Mount Gerizim and Mount Ebal (Josh. 8:33).

ARK OF THE COVENANT[1]

God directs His people at this time through the movement of the ark of the covenant. When they see it moving, carried by the priests and Levites, they are to follow—at a reverent distance of about one thousand yards (3:3, 4). Beyond waiting for the ark to move, Joshua directs the people to prepare to move forward with the Lord: "Sanctify yourselves" (v. 5). Although the Israelites had come out of Egypt, they still had some of Egypt left in them, and they needed to jettison that and to devote themselves fully to the Lord.

What steps did the people take to sanctify themselves? (see Ex. 19:14–15)

BIBLE EXTRA

Sanctification—the setting apart of oneself physically and spiritually for God's holy purposes—is always the first step to receive God's promises. Explore New Testament teaching on the practical ways believers are to sanctify themselves in Paul's first letter to the Thessalonian believers. List what you discover:

1 Thess. 3:12–13; 4:9–10

1 Thess. 4:3

1 Thess. 4:4–5

1 Thess. 4:6

1 Thess. 4:11

1 Thess. 4:12

The flooded Jordan River lies directly in the path of the Israelites, and crossing it is humanly impossible. But God has sent His people to this place, and He will direct them through this barrier.

By what authority did Joshua direct the priests carrying the ark to enter the Jordan? (vv. 6, 8)

 FAITH ALIVE

Read Romans 10:17, and write from it what produces biblical faith:

Despite all the differences in time and circumstance between you and Joshua, how may you today live the same life of faith that is portrayed in Joshua 3?

Besides moving His people into the Promised Land, what

two other results does God accomplish through the miraculous crossing of the Jordan?

1. (v. 7)

2. (vv. 9–10)

Reflect on v. 7. What divine gift is essential for anyone to lead others spiritually?

Who are the seven enemies that Israel will encounter in the Promised Land? (v. 10)

God has directed Joshua, Joshua and the officers have instructed the people, and all the Israelites are on the move. At what moment does their obedience to God's word meet with the sight of God's miracle actually occurring? (vv. 14, 15)

 FAITH ALIVE

Imagine that you are part of the Israelites, perhaps a priest helping move the ark. You are approaching this flooded river, step by step, without seeing anything change—the river continues to be swollen and rushes downstream. What thoughts and emotions might conflict within you as you keep approaching the apparently unchanging river?

What one fact in this situation keeps it from being the madness of a misled people marching, lemming-like, toward suicide? (vv. 9–13)

As the story of Rahab illustrates (2:1–24), faith requires active obedience to the word of God. What if the priests had feared the swollen stream more than they believed in God and believed that He had spoken to Joshua and had therefore refused to step into the river?

Name an occasion when you had received clear direction from God, yet your fear of circumstances or the possible outcome fought against your desire to trust God and obey Him.

Is there a promise God has spoken to you that requires you to act in order to receive the promise? What action is God calling for? Why wait any longer to obey?

PROBING THE DEPTHS

The passage of the Israelites across the Jordan River on dry ground raises an interesting question about the nature of miracles. The damming of the Jordan can also be explained in natural terms. Earthquakes are common in this area, and in 1927 an earthquake triggered a mudslide near Adam that interrupted the river's flow for twenty-one hours. Such a temporary dam is possibly what caused the Jordan to stop flowing nineteen miles downstream at the time Israel crossed over.

The miraculous nature of the event is not diminished by proposing such natural means. God's supernatural sense of timing is still required. A landslide and subsequent damming of the river upstream would need to occur many hours before. Then, at the exact moment when the priests stepped into the river, the flow of water stopped. Similarly, after Israel had crossed over, when the priests emerged from the riverbed, the flow of water immediately resumed. The temporary dam upstream had given way, and the torrent of water arrived downstream just as Israel was safely across. Thus Israel's need for safe passage was miraculously provided by God at the exact moment it was required.[2]

Has God ever answered your prayer with natural means, but with supernatural timing?

What events had transpired beforehand so that your answer to prayer arrived right on time?

A REMINDER OF GOD'S PROMISE (JOSH. 4:1–24)

After the people of Israel cross the Jordan River, Joshua himself erects a memorial using twelve stones on the spot where the priests had stood with the ark. These stones were still visible, undoubtedly during a period of low flow, when the author of Joshua was writing! Then a representative from each of the twelve tribes carries a stone from the riverbed to the camp. With these stones Joshua later erects a memorial at Gilgal, which now becomes the site of the permanent Israelite camp in Canaan. When the priests carrying the ark of the covenant emerge from the riverbed, the flood of water resumes.

What statement did the memorial of stones make to future generations? (Josh. 4:6–7, 22–23)

To the peoples of the earth? (Josh. 4:24)

Why do you think it is important that each generation has memorials of God's activity?

    WORD WEALTH

The Hebrew word *'abar* occurs twenty-one times in chapters 3–4, where it is translated "cross(ed) over," "passed," or "carried over."[3] The repetition of this verb shows its importance in this section. Seven groups or things are said to make this important crossing over the Jordan River. List the verses in chapters 3—4 where this verb is found.

The people (Israel)

The priests

The ark

The twelve men

The twelve stones

The men of Reuben, Gad, and Manasseh

The 40,000 warriors

BEHIND THE SCENES

In Joshua 4:9 the author of Joshua inserts the parenthetical comment that Joshua's memorial can still be seen in his day. This is the first of seven times where he declares that some evidence of Joshua's conquest is still visible in his day. Such statements lend historical credibility to his account. Look up the following references in Joshua, and name the seven evidences that still existed in the author's day.

4:9

6:25

7:26

8:29

9:27

14:14

16:10

BIBLE EXTRA

Memorial stones were erected on several other occasions in the Old Testament. Look up these Scripture references and record why the memorial was set up on each occasion.

Jacob at Bethel (Gen. 28:18–22)

Jacob at Mizpah (Gen. 31:45–53)

Joshua at Shechem (Josh. 24:26–27)

Samuel near Mizpah (1 Sam. 7:12)

FAITH ALIVE

Today spiritual memorials are still important, especially for the sake of our children and grandchildren. Such memorials—either occasions or things—remind us how God intervened at some previous time. Mother's Day is such an occasion in our family because on that day both my wife and I became Christians. Another memorial around our household is the old Jeep Wagoneer that we still drive. It reminds us of God's miraculous provision when we desperately needed a vehicle. The next time God does something wonderful in your life, consider making a memorial to recall his gracious provision.

Do you have special times or possessions that recall God's miraculous deeds in your life?

List two or three memorials that you might make now.

BEHIND THE SCENES

Gilgal, from the Hebrew word *galal,* can mean either "circle (as of stones)" or "rolling."[4] In its first meaning Gilgal was the location of the memorial made of stones from the Jordan River (Josh. 4:20). In its second meaning God rolled away the reproach of Egypt when the Israelites were circumcised at Gilgal (Josh. 5:9). Gilgal was the site of the first Israelite camp in the Promised Land and the base of operations for its conquest. The city was likewise significant in the nation's later history. It was one of three cities where Samuel sat as a judge (1 Sam. 7:16) and thus served as the spiritual capital where all the people assembled (1 Sam. 10:8; 13:4–8). Saul was made the king at Gilgal (1 Sam. 11:14–15). And David was welcomed back as king there after he defeated Absalom (2 Sam. 19:15, 40). At Gilgal Elisha performed his miracle of purifying the pot of poisonous stew (2 Kin. 4:38–41).

BECOMING HEIRS OF ABRAHAM'S PROMISE (JOSH. 5:1–15)

Because no male children born during the wilderness period had been circumcised, God now commands that every male, both young and old, be circumcised at Gilgal. God's promise of land to Abraham was conditioned by his submission to circumcision. Before this generation of Israelites can receive Abraham's promise, they must likewise submit to circumcision. Following the circumcision, Israel celebrates the first Passover in the Promised Land. Suddenly the supply of manna that has sustained Israel for forty years ceases, and the Israelites must begin to eat the food of the land. Near Jericho Joshua meets a mysterious figure with a sword who identifies himself as the Commander of the army of the Lord.

Why had the generation that wandered in the wilderness for forty years failed to circumcise their sons? (Josh. 5:6)

Where was the first Jewish feast celebrated in the Promised Land? (Josh. 5:10–11)

What circumstance prompted God to cease providing manna to the people of Israel? (Josh. 5:11–12)

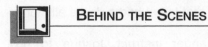

BEHIND THE SCENES

According to the covenant that God made with Abraham (Gen. 17:10–14), every male descendant was to be circumcised on the eighth day. Abraham became circumcised when he was ninety-nine years old; his son Ishmael was thirteen years old (Gen. 17:24–25). Isaac's circumcision is mentioned (Gen. 21:4), while Jacob's is not. One reason why Pharaoh's daughter could identify baby Moses as a Hebrew was because he was circumcised (Ex. 2:6). God tried to kill Moses for failing to circumcise his firstborn son. This forced his wife Zipporah to circumcise Gershom, a duty she apparently detested (Ex. 4:24–26). Moses promised a day when the external circumcision would give way to a circumcision of the heart, wherein the people of Israel would love God with all their heart (Deut. 30:6).

In the New Testament circumcision is no longer an indication of a person's covenant relationship with God (Acts 15:1, 19–21; Gal. 2:3; 3:28). Without faith expressing itself in obedience, circumcision means nothing (Rom. 2:25–29). The New Testament does refer to spiritual circumcision, the putting off of the sinful flesh so that the new man might be raised with Christ (Col. 2:11–12).

PROBING THE DEPTHS

Who was the Commander of the army of the Lord whom Joshua met outside of Jericho—Jesus Christ or an archangel? Several clues help us to identify him. The drawn sword in his hand is reminiscent of the Angel of the Lord who confronted both Balaam (Num. 22:23) and David (1 Chr. 21:16) with a drawn sword. Yet the Commander allowed Joshua to worship Him, unlike angels who do not allow people to worship them (see Rev. 19:10). These clues suggest that the figure was divine, an appearance of the second member of the Trinity before His incarnation. The Commander's appearance undoubtedly assured Joshua that Israel had a divine ally for its upcoming battles.

What did the Commander instruct Joshua to do? (Josh. 5:15)

What command did the Lord give to Moses at the burning bush? (Ex. 3:5)

CAPTURING THE FIRST PROMISED CITY (JOSH. 6:1–27)

Jericho is the first major city that the Israelites encounter in the Promised Land. Because of the two spies, the king of Jericho is prepared for an imminent attack. Before the battle God pronounces victory before announcing his unorthodox strategy to destroy the city—Joshua is to conduct praise marches around the city! As in the crossing of the Jordan, the priests with their trumpets are to lead the people. The perfect number seven assumes symbolic importance, perhaps because of the divine week of creation (Gen. 2:2–3). Its fourteen uses (twice seven) in this chapter speak of seven priests, seven days, and seven journeys around the city wall. The Israelites faithfully execute the divine battle plan, and when their shout is raised following the signal from the priests, Jericho's walls collapse, just as God said they would! In this first battle of God's Holy War against the Canaanites only Rahab and her family are saved.

Name the tasks related to Jericho's defeat that were assigned to each group of Israelites.

The armed men (vv. 3, 9)

The priests (vv. 4, 6)

The people (vv. 5, 10)

The spies (vv. 22–23)

All the Israelites (vv. 21, 24)

What was the place of the ark in the battle? (4:4, 6–13)

BIBLE EXTRA

Jericho, known as the City of Palms, is perhaps the oldest city on earth—over 8,000 years old. Its site in the Jordan Valley is also the lowest spot in the world at 800 feet below sea level.[5] The biblical description of the Canaanite walled cities suggests that they were large communities. On the contrary, Jericho sat on approximately seven acres of land. To walk around its walls would not take a long time. Thus the vanguard of the Israelites would return to camp long before the rearguard had circled the walls. Most of the inhabitants of ancient cities lived outside the walls, attending to their flocks and fields. Only when an enemy approached would they retreat behind the defenses of the city's high stone walls. Hence, at the approach of the Israelites "Jericho was securely shut up; . . . none went out, and none came in" (Josh. 6:1). The construction of the typical double wall utilized by Jericho and the other Canaanite cities is shown in the following illustration.

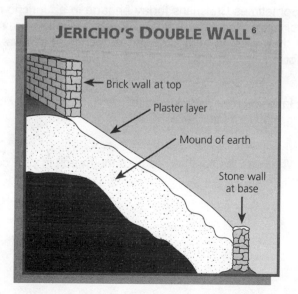

JERICHO'S DOUBLE WALL[6]

Brick wall at top

Plaster layer

Mound of earth

Stone wall at base

PROBING THE DEPTHS

"And the walls came a-tumblin' down" is a line from a familiar African-American spiritual. But how did these walls, more than forty feet high and perhaps sixty-six feet wide, come crashing down? Some people have suggested a natural explanation, like a massive earthquake.[6] Present-day earthquakes in California and Iran certainly demonstrate the destructiveness of large-scale seismic activity.

God had already used an earthquake to punish Korah and his family (Num. 16:31–32). If this was His method at Jericho, the issue is one of timing, like the possible damming of the Jordan River. But it also concerns location because the Israelites outside the walls were left unharmed. If an earthquake did destroy the walls, its epicenter was localized only under Jericho itself, and miraculously the seismic shock did not radiate outward as is normal.

FAITH ALIVE

Sometimes Christians today engage in a "Jericho march" by encircling a strategic spiritual target. Through prayer and praise they seek to neutralize the demonic influences and to see God's kingdom established in their place.

Have you ever participated in such a march, and what was the target of your intercession?

What was the spiritual result of the march in your community and church?

WORD WEALTH

The trumpets that the priests blew around the city were not made of metal, but rather of rams' horns. These shofars (Heb. *shopharim*) cannot be considered musical instruments because they could make only a few notes. Rather, they were military signaling instruments that produced a loud, intimidating sound. They were used to assemble the army (Judg. 3:27; 1 Sam. 13:3), to sound an attack (Job 39:24–25), and to sound an alarm (Jer. 6:1; Amos 3:6).[7] The priests' blowing of seven shofars on the seventh day following seven laps around the city was intended to frighten the inhabitants of Jericho and break their will.

FAITH ALIVE

Joshua had seen Israel's response to the report of the spies following their mission in Canaan. The murmuring and complaining that resulted had caused Israel to wander forty years in the wilderness (Num. 14:1–38). Although it is unstated in the narrative, this is possibly why Joshua enforced silence on the people during the seven-day siege of Jericho.

Why is it important to focus on and speak only God's promises during a spiritual battle?

What effect does negative speech have on your faith and the faith of those around you?

BEHIND THE SCENES

As the Israelites stood before the charred rubble of Jericho, Joshua pronounced a curse on anyone who would rebuild the city (Josh. 6:26). Whoever laid the foundation again and rebuilt the city gates would lose both his firstborn and his youngest son. Jericho was soon resettled (Josh 18:21; Judg. 3:13; 2 Sam. 10:5), but apparently not as a walled city. Some 500 years later Hiel, a resident of Bethel, rebuilt the city as a fortress (1 Kin. 16:34). He disregarded warnings about Joshua's curse, perhaps considering it a superstition. The result was tragic, with his eldest son Abiram and his youngest son Segub dying during the reconstruction. The lesson is clear: to disregard the divinely inspired word of a prophet will bring painful consequences, no matter how long it takes!

 ## Faith Alive

Unlike the previous generation whose "grasshopper mentality" had prevented them from going into the land (Num. 13:33), their children believed that their God was bigger than the giants and the walls of Jericho that loomed ahead. Even though the battle had not yet been engaged, Joshua confessed victory (Josh. 6:16) because of what the Lord had already promised him (Josh. 6:2). Through his confession this anointed leader demonstrated faith in God's ability to fulfill His word.

What promise has God made to you for which you need to confess victory?

The challenges you face may be enormous. Biblical faith does not ask us to pretend that problems do not exist. Instead, faith compels us to focus on the God who is greater than any and all problems. We worship God when we rehearse His great deeds—all the ways He has saved His people throughout Bible times and throughout our life and times. In worship God strengthens our faith—our informed confidence in His victory and the trust in Him that propels us to act on His word to us. In this process, where do you stand now?

• Worshiping—remembering God's acts of faithfulness—so I will trust Him more

• Confirming God's specific direction for me—hearing from God through Scripture, prayer, and counsel from spiritual leaders

• Acting on what I've heard from God—joyfully, tenaciously, assertively

What is the next step God wants you to take?

1. Ark of the Covenant, *Spirit-Filled Life® Bible* (Nashville: Thomas Nelson Publishers, 1991), 137, "The Furniture of the Tabernacle."

2. Donald H. Madvig, "Joshua," *Expositor's Bible Commentary,* Vol. 3 (Grand Rapids: Zondervan Publishing House), 272.

3. *Spirit-Filled Life® Bible,* 309–10, "Word Wealth: Joshua 3:4, passed."

4. *The Illustrated Bible Dictionary,* Vol. 2 (Wheaton: Tyndale House Publishers), 562, "Gilgal."

5. *Nelson's New Illustrated Bible Dictionary* (Nashville: Thomas Nelson Publishers, 1995), 647–48, "Jericho."

6. *Word in Life Study Bible* (Nashville: Thomas Nelson Publishers, 1996), 401–2, "The Wall of Jericho."

7. *Nelson's New Illustrated Bible Dictionary,* 871, "Musical Instruments of the Bible, Trumpet."

Lesson 3/Hindrances to Possessing God's Promise
Joshua 7:1—9:27

Things often are not as they appear. Israel and others throughout history have learned this lesson to their sorrow.

Homer's epic poem, *The Iliad*, describes one of the greatest deceptions of all time. When Queen Helen of Sparta was kidnapped, the Greeks set siege to Troy in order to rescue her. The war dragged out for years, with neither side able to gain a decisive victory. Finally, to break the deadlock, Odysseus proposed that the Greeks build a giant wooden horse and hide their fiercest warriors inside. The rest of the fighters would sail away, leaving the impression that they had returned to Greece.

Thus one morning the Trojans found the huge horse abandoned on the beach. Several of their number pleaded with their countrymen to destroy the horse, but a Greek informer, left behind to mislead the Trojans, successfully convinced them to drag the horse into the city. That night, after the residents of Troy had collapsed from their victory parties, the Greeks inside the horse lowered themselves from its belly and signaled the naval fleet to return. When the city gates were opened, the Greeks poured in and quickly overcame the unsuspecting inhabitants. Thanks to their trick, the Greeks were finally triumphant.

The Israelites, like the Trojans, also became victims of a deception. While not as dramatic as the Trojan horse, the ploy of the Gibeonites likewise succeeded. Because Joshua and the leaders failed to inquire of the Lord, Israel was forced to live for generations with the consequences of the deception.

THE HINDRANCE OF OVERCONFIDENCE (JOSH. 7:1–9)

The quick defeat of Jericho apparently sparked an attitude in the Israelites that the conquest of Canaan was going to be easy. When Joshua sends spies to check out the city of Ai, their reply suggests an overconfidence regarding the task. Consequently only a portion of Israel's troops are dispatched, but they are easily defeated with the loss of thirty-six lives. The defeat provokes a spirit of fear and cowardice throughout the Israelite camp. The response of Joshua and the elders is to repent by tearing their clothing and putting dust on their heads. They spend all day before the ark of the covenant seeking God.

What was the spies' assessment of the city of Ai? (Josh. 7:3)

What was the Israelites' reaction to the defeat? (Josh. 7:5)

What was Joshua's reaction to the defeat? (Josh. 7:7)

What was Joshua's concern regarding God's name? (Josh. 7:9)

 FAITH ALIVE

Sometimes, when our prayers are quickly or easily answered, we begin to think that we had some role in bringing about the answer. The next time we pray, we may try to put God in a box by making Him answer the same way.

Why do you think God changes his methods and ways of answering our prayers?

What has God taught you about how He answers your prayers?

THE HINDRANCE OF GREED (JOSH. 7:10–26)

God informs Joshua that a secret sin is responsible for Israel's defeat at Ai. One of the Israelites had disregarded orders and had taken some of the spoils from Jericho. Before Israel can move forward, the guilty party must be removed from their midst. Joshua commands the people to sanctify themselves and to gather in a sacred assembly on the following morning. Through a system of lots the guilty family is finally identified, and Achan is named as the culprit. Because of greed, he took some spoils and hid them under his tent. The death penalty is meted out not only upon Achan, but upon his family and livestock, and a heap of stones raised over their graves as a memorial for Israel.

What is the cause for God's displeasure with the Israelites? (Josh. 7:13)

What had Achan's greed prompted him to take from Jericho? (Josh. 7:21)

Who also participated in the judgment upon Achan? (Josh. 7:24)

What was the punishment meted out to Achan and the rest? (Josh. 7:25)

 FAITH ALIVE

The valley where Achan's sin was discovered and punished was later called the Valley of Achor, which in Hebrew means "trouble." Whenever the Israelites would later cross the valley and see Achan's grave, they would recall his sin and its damage to the nation. The reminder would deter others from falling into similar sins and thereby incurring God's divine judgment.

Looking back at your own spiritual journey, can you identify any Achor valleys where you encountered trouble moving into the promises of God?

What sins or temptations did you have to put to death before you could continue?

BIBLE EXTRA

In Joshua 7:12 God vows to withdraw His presence from Israel. This promise of His presence, first given to Joshua in chapter 1:5–9, is even more foundational than the promise of land. He likewise gave this promise to Moses at the burning bush (Ex. 3:12). His ultimatum to Joshua boils down to this choice: does Israel want the presence of God or the presence of the accursed objects more?

What do the Israelites pray for Joshua regarding God's divine presence? (Josh. 1:17)

How does God show Israel that Joshua was exalted to a place of leadership? (Josh. 3:7)

What is the sign for Israel that she will possess the land by driving out her enemies? (Josh. 3:10)

WORD WEALTH

Doomed (Heb. *cherem*) "refers to the cultic dedication of these men and things, so that God, not man, receives glory and profit."[1] Thus every living thing in Jericho—both man and beast—was doomed to destruction. Only metal vessels were to be spared for use in the treasury of the Lord's house. The curse upon these living things was transferred to the greedy Achan and through him to all of Israel.

The Septuagint, the Greek translation of the Old Testament, uses the word *anathema* here, which likewise means "accursed" or "separated." In the New Testament Paul pronounced an anathema, or curse, on those who were preaching a false gospel to the Galatians (Gal. 1:8–9). In the early church an anathema "was applied to a person expelled from the church because of moral offenses or persistence in heresy."[2]

PROBING THE DEPTHS

To our modern perspective the total annihilation of people and animals in the Canaanite cities seems quite barbaric. How could a God of love condemn so many to death? The answer is not an easy one, but relates to God's essential nature and character. God is a God of love and of justice. Canaanite civilization was idolatrous and immoral, with practices such as ritual prostitution and the sacrifice of infants. God used the Israelites to exact judgment on this civilization. He knew that if the Canaanites were allowed to remain and intermix with the Israelites, His people would be compromised and unable to follow His commandments. The subsequent history of Israel validates this concern. The heathen peoples that remained in the Promised Land continually placed the stumbling blocks of idolatry and immorality in the path of the Israelites.

Does the church today have the right and obligation to use force to implement the commandments and will of God? Why or why not?

How do militaristic religious movements such as the Crusades warn us about the dangers of enacting such a policy?

The New Testament perspective clearly indicates that "our struggle is not a quest for dominance which employs a political or military means."[3] Yet is there a place for judgment in the church? Paul provides a helpful perspective on this issue in his first letter to the Corinthians. A member of the Corinthian church is guilty of a sexual affair with his father's wife and refuses to repent of the relationship (1 Cor. 5:1–2). Paul admonishes the Corinthians to judge the brother by putting him outside the congregation (1 Cor. 5:13). The apostle quotes here an injunction found repeatedly in the Old Testament (Deut. 13:5; 17:7, 12; 19:19; 21:21; 22:21, 24; 24:7). In its context in Deuteronomy the offending party is to be stoned to death by the Israelites. In its New Testament context the guilty person is not to be killed, but to be excommunicated and handed over to Satan. Such judgment is to be for redemption and salvation (1 Cor. 5:5). Excommunication was apparently responsible for the subsequent restoration of this brother to fellowship with the church (2 Cor. 2:3–11). Why do you think Paul saw the disfellowshiping and handing over to Satan of the guilty brother as divine judgment?

Does your church have a disciplinary policy for handling members who refuse to repent of sin?

BEHIND THE SCENES

One way in which the Jews determined the will of God was to cast the sacred lot. Solomon expressed the common belief that the decision of the lot was from the Lord (Prov. 16:33). How the lot was used precisely remains unknown. Probably some small object like a stone or piece of wood was marked to give a yes or no answer.

Joshua used the lot to determine the guilty party, who was somehow "taken" by God (Josh. 7:15). The field of possible candidates was gradually narrowed until only one choice remained. In this case the tribes were narrowed to clans, then to families, then to households, and finally to an individual. This same process was repeated when Saul was chosen as king (1 Sam. 10:20–21) and when Jonathan's guilt was determined (1 Sam. 14:41–42). Lots were used again in Joshua 15—21 to determine the tribal inheritances in the land of Canaan. The single use of lots by the disciples occurs when Matthias is chosen by lot to succeed Judas (Acts 1:26). The coming of the Holy Spirit with His ability to impart divine knowledge and counsel seems to have eliminated the further need for lots in the early church.[4]

Have you ever attempted to find a shortcut to God's will by devising a Christian version of a lot? What was the result?

In what way(s) does the practice of opening the Bible and pointing to a particular verse for guidance resemble the lot?

What should be the Christian attitude toward gaining God's promised blessings through gambling and lottery tickets?

TAKING THE SECOND PROMISED CITY (JOSH. 8:1–35)

With the sin of Achan behind them, the Israelites reattempt to take the city of Ai. Their confidence is now in the Lord rather than in themselves, and His presence is once again with them. This time God tells Joshua to take the whole army, and He allows the Israelites to take the livestock and material goods as booty. Joshua devises a tactical ambush in which the strategy is to trick the inhabitants of Ai. While an Israelite contingent fakes a retreat to draw the Canaanites out of their fortress, the main Israelite force now occupies the city from their hiding place behind it. Its twelve thousand residents—doomed to destruction—are all killed, and the captured city is then burned. The king of Ai is hanged before Joshua, and at sunset his body is cut down and buried beneath a heap of stones. Following Ai's destruction Joshua takes the Israelites northward to Mount Ebal where he builds an altar to the Lord. With half of the nation on Mount Ebal and the other half on Mount Gerizim Joshua renews the covenant with the assembly of the Israelites.

Why do you think God changed the terms of the booty for this battle? (Josh. 8:2)

Of what sin were the residents of Ai themselves now guilty, so that they left their city open and unguarded? (Josh. 8:16–17)

What would be the future significance of the heap of stones at Ai's entrance gate under which the king was buried? (Josh. 8:29)

Why was it necessary that everyone, including the children and strangers such as Rahab and her family, be present for the covenant renewal at Ebal and Gerizim? (Josh. 8:33)

  BEHIND THE SCENES

The covenant ceremony that Joshua renews with the Israelites was prescribed by Moses before his death. Deuteronomy 27 lists twelve curses that the Levites are to read and to which the Israelites are to answer responsively by saying "Amen." Several of the curses find their parallel in the Ten Commandments (Ex. 20:1–17). Deuteronomy 28 goes on to list the blessings that the tribes of Simeon, Levi, Judah, Issachar, Joseph, and Benjamin were to speak from Mount Gerizim, and the curses that the tribes of Reuben, Gad, Asher, Zebulun, Dan, and Naphtali were to speak from Mount Ebal. Unlike the curses previously named, those listed in chapter 28 provide frightening details on how they will be carried out. The heart of the blessings is found in the four "Blesseds" (Deut. 28:3–6). These focus

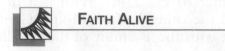
particularly on the prosperous quality of life which the Israelites will enjoy in the Promised Land.

 FAITH ALIVE

The Lord is the God of the second chance. Even though the Israelites messed up their first attempt to take Ai, after their repentance God gave them a second chance.

Can you name a time when God gave you a second chance to make a situation right?

What spiritual changes did you have to make before God gave you that second chance?

 BEHIND THE SCENES

Moses also commanded the Israelites to do two other things. On Mount Ebal they were to erect a memorial of stones whitewashed in lime upon which are written God's commandments (Deut. 27:2–4, 8). Nearby they were also to build an altar of unhewn stones upon which burnt offerings and peace offerings are to be sacrificed (Deut. 27:5–6). When Joshua arrived at Ebal, he immediately constructed the unhewn altar and wrote the Law of Moses on the stones (Josh. 8:30–32).

 FAITH ALIVE

Why do you think God required that altars be made of stones upon which no person had ever used an iron tool?

What sort of altars are you constructing—of hewn or unhewn stones?

THE HINDRANCE OF SELF-SUFFICIENCY (JOSH. 9:1–27)

The fall of Jericho and Ai brought an immediate reaction from the kings in Canaan who formed an alliance to fight the Israelites. The city of Gibeon, however, decided upon a different strategy—one of deception—to deal with the enemy. One day a ragged group of Gibeonites appeared in the Israelite camp at Gilgal. They claimed to have traveled a great distance in order to make a covenant with the Israelites, whose God was noted for His might and power. Joshua and the rulers looked at the Gibeonites' sorry condition and immediately believed their story. They made a covenant of peace with their enemy without consulting the Lord.

Soon the self-sufficient Israelites learned that they had been deceived by a confederation of Hivite cities that was supposed to be destroyed. Although the Israelites complained, their rulers rightly stood by their oath. However, because of their deception, Joshua cursed them and made them slaves throughout future generations. In spite of subjugation, the Gibeonites were happy to be alive because all their neighbors were soon to be destroyed.

How did the Gibeonites successfully execute their deception? (Josh. 9:4–5)

What motivated the Gibeonites to ask for a treaty? (Josh. 9:9–10)

Why do you think the Israelites failed to consult God? (Josh. 9:14)

What was the reaction of the Israelites when they learned of the deception, and why did they not break the covenant? (Josh. 9:18–20)

What role was consigned to the Gibeonites in the Israelite camp? (Josh. 9:21, 27)

FAITH ALIVE

This story illustrates the trouble that can result when we make decisions based on outward appearances rather than on revelation from the Holy Spirit. The first three gifts of the Holy Spirit are related particularly to spiritual insight—the word of wisdom, the word of knowledge, and the discerning of spirits (1 Cor. 12:8). God promises to give us wisdom when we need it—but first we must ask! (James 1:5)

Can you recall a time when spiritual self-sufficiency likewise got you into trouble?

What lessons did the Lord teach you as a result of that experience?

How do you involve God in your decision making each day?

BEHIND THE SCENES

Gibeon, located six miles northwest of Jerusalem, was the chief city of the Hivites. Three other cities were allied with it—Chephirah, Beeroth, and Kirjath Jearim. Gibeon is best noted for its deception of the Israelites and the subsequent battle near it when Joshua commanded the moon and sun to stand still. It was later the site of a bloody contest of strength between twelve of David's men and twelve men of Ishbosheth. After the men killed one another at "the Field of the Sharp Swords," David's forces triumphed in the battle that followed (2 Sam. 2:12–17). Gibeon became a high place for sacrifice, and here Solomon asked for wisdom when God appeared to him in a dream (1 Kin. 3:4–9). Jeremiah mentions a great pool In Gibeon (Jer. 41:12). This pool, cut out of solid rock, was discovered by archaeologists in 1956. Its upper shaft is thirty-five feet deep and thirty-seven feet in diameter. A stairway extends down through this upper shaft into a lower chamber that descends another forty-five feet to groundwater. The tremendous effort expended to construct this pool shows the importance of water for the survival of cities in ancient Israel.[5] The failure of Israel to occupy the Gibeonite cities brought long-term consequences. These cities sat along the main north-south road and thus prevented the unification of the tribes in the land. This later contributed to Israel's division into the northern and southern kingdoms.

1. Trent C. Butler, *Joshua,* Word Biblical Commentary (Waco: Word Book Publishers, 1983), 71.

2. *Nelson's New Illustrated Bible Dictionary* (Nashville: Thomas Nelson Publishers, 1995), 54, "Anathema."

3. *Hayford's Bible Handbook* (Nashville: Thomas Nelson Publishers, 1995), 45, "Kingdom Key."

4. *Nelson's New Illustrated Bible Dictionary,* 774–75, "Lots, Casting of."

5. Ibid., 492–93, "Gibeon."

Lesson 4/Fighting for God's Promise
Joshua 10:1—12:24

"As long as the grasses grow and the rivers flow"—the United States government treaty in 1868 guaranteed the Sioux Indian nation possession of their land forever. When gold was discovered in the Black Hills just a few years later, however, miners poured in to stake their claim. The U.S. Army did nothing to prevent this illegal incursion of miners on Indian territory. In fact, when the Indians acted in self-defense to try to keep intruders out, the government used such Indian "atrocities" as an excuse to send troops into the area to "protect" the miners. The defeat of General Custer in 1876 proved to be a hollow victory in the Indians' futile attempt to defend their homeland. Subsequent treaty negotiations forced the Sioux to cede their sacred "Paha Sapa" (Black Hills) to the white man.

The failure of the United States to live up to its treaty promises is one of the black marks in American history. In fact, this broken treaty has never been resolved: the Sioux Indians are still trying to get back the Black Hills. Such broken covenants made by a supposedly Christian government are one probable reason that Native Americans have been resistant to the gospel.

This lesson underscores the importance of a treaty in God's sight. When Joshua made a covenant to protect the Gibeonites, he never suspected that Israelite lives soon would be put on the line for these Canaanite people that were supposed to have been killed. When the Amorites attacked the Gibeonites, Joshua honored his covenant. In defending Gibeon he secured Israel's mightiest victory and received his greatest miracle. Such divine blessing indicates the importance God places on the commitments of His people, even those made through deception!

THE AMORITE COUNTERATTACK (JOSH. 10:1–27)

The destruction of Jericho and Ai coupled with the surrender of the powerful city of Gibeon spells great trouble for the other kings in Canaan. Strategically the Israelite invasion was driving a wedge between their northern and southern kingdoms. Therefore the king of Jerusalem makes an alliance with four other Amorite kings to repel the Israelites. The combined armies advance against Gibeon in order to punish this city for its defection and to lure Joshua into battle. For the kings realized that the treaty bound the Israelites to defend Gibeon if it were attacked. Joshua indeed comes to the city's rescue and, despite an all-night march, his troops rout the Amorites. As the enemy forces retreat, God's wrath also falls upon them, and more Canaanites are killed by hailstones than by combat. As mopping-up operations continue, Joshua and his army literally run out of daylight. Then, in a remarkable operation of faith, Joshua commands the sun and moon to stand still. And God remarkably overrules the forces of nature and answers Joshua's prayer so that vengeance against His enemies is completed. The five Amorite kings, like the king of Ai, are hung from trees and their bodies cut down before sunset. If they are left longer, the land would be defiled (Deut. 21:23). The corpses are thrown into the same cave in which they hid, and rocks are piled up to seal the entrance. This is another memorial of the Israelite conquest that could be seen until the author's day.

What king organized the resistance to the Israelites? (Josh. 10:1)

What five Amorite cities made an alliance? (Josh. 10:3, 5)

Over what cities did the sun and moon stand still? (Josh. 10:12–13)

What was so special about Joshua's actions regarding the sun and moon? (Josh. 10:14)

PROBING THE DEPTHS

The miracle of the sun and moon standing still for about a day is denied by many biblical scholars. They argue that such an event is scientifically impossible. If the rotation of the earth stopped for a day, there would be chaos in the solar system. What actually happened then? Several explanations have been proposed—an eclipse of the sun, an extended cloud cover for relief from the heat, a morning mist that lingered longer than normal.[1] Other scholars explain away the quotation from the Book of Jasher as simply poetic description, not literal fact. With the damming of the Jordan and the collapse of Jericho's wall, we suggested that natural means were possibly involved. However, with the immobilization of the sun and moon, any natural explanation is impossible given the laws governing the solar system. It is all supernatural. While we can understand the scientific improbability of the event, we also recognize that the God who made the solar system can intervene at His discretion. It is best to accept the miracle and conclude with the author: "And there has been no day like that, before it or after it" (Josh. 10:14).

FAITH ALIVE

Joshua's command to the sun and moon demonstrates what in the New Testament is called the gift of faith. When he speaks directly to the two natural sources of light, he is in fact speaking to the God who created them. Paul called the gift of faith one of the nine gifts of the Holy Spirit (1 Cor. 12:9; 13:2). Jesus Himself spoke about a faith that was able to move a mountain and cast it into the sea (Mark 11:23). He taught this in the context of cursing a fig tree for its failure to produce fruit. Both illustrations are drawn from nature and suggest a supernatural, God-given faith that is distinct from the normal, everyday faith of the Christian life (Rom. 1:17). The gift of faith is available to all Christians for those "mission impossible" situations when only immediate supernatural intervention will resolve the problem.

Have you ever exercised the gift of faith to resolve an impossible situation? When?

In what area(s) do you believe God might be wanting you to exercise the gift of faith?

 ## At A Glance

The topography of Israel plays an important role in this conflict. The battle at Gibeon begins on the Judean plateau northwest of Jerusalem at an altitude of approximately 2500 feet. To reach Gibeon, Joshua and his men must first make a forced overnight march, climbing approximately 3300 feet from the Jordan Valley. Despite their exhaustion, the Israelites receive strength from God to engage the Amorites. Fortunately for the Israelites it was "all downhill" for their enemies after that. The Amorite retreat followed the descent along the ridge of Beth Horon into the Aijalon Valley to the west. The final Amorite defeat took place at Azekah and Makkedah, cities in a region of western foothills called the Shephelah. These cities were over a thousand feet lower than Gibeon. Not only was the longer day a factor in Israel's victory, but the favorable terrain for pursuit was strategically important.

 ## Faith Alive

Not long ago, people could simply give their word or shake hands on something, and the deal was done. Today even formal contracts are often worth little more than the paper they are written on. Keeping one's word is an important aspect of integrity, as demonstrated by Joshua and his defense of the Gibeonites.

When you give your word to people, can they rely on you to fulfill it?

If you have trouble following through with your commitments, what lifestyle changes can you make to become more reliable?

 ## BEHIND THE SCENES

The authors of the Old Testament occasionally cite other books that served as their sources for information. One of these is the Book of Jasher, or Book of the Upright. Joshua 10:12–13 contains a poem from this book that describes how the sun and moon stopped so that Israel could triumph over her enemies. Second Samuel 1:19–27 records a lamentation of David from the Book of Jasher called the Song of the Bow. This poem laments the tragic deaths of Saul and his son Jonathan on Mount Gilboa. Jasher was apparently an ancient Israelite poet who celebrated the victories of Israel's heroes in his epic poetry. In recognition of this, the New King James Version sets both passages in poetic form.

BEHIND THE SCENES

In verse 24 Joshua summons his captains and instructs them to put their feet on the necks of the five kings. This ancient custom was meant not only to humiliate these captives but to symbolize the total victory that God would give Israel over her enemies. This subjugation fulfilled Noah's prophecy that Canaan would someday be the servant of Shem (Gen. 9:25–27). King David was likewise a great warrior who put his enemies under the soles of his feet (1 Kings 5:5). David used this image in his great messianic psalm where he writes, "The LORD said to my Lord,/ 'Sit at My right hand,/ Till I make Your enemies Your footstool' " (Ps. 110:1).

This is one of the most quoted verses in the New Testament. Jesus demonstrates from this verse that He is superior to David (see Matt. 22:44). On the Day of Pentecost Peter quotes Psalm 110 to prove that Christ did indeed rise victorious over the grave. Following His ascension Jesus now sits at the right hand of God in heaven. If this were not so, the Holy Spirit could not have been poured out (Acts 2:33–35).

The implications of this verse for spiritual warfare are staggering. Satan has been defeated and cast out of heaven (Luke 10:18; Rev. 12:9, 10). Jesus has now given believers authority to trample over the enemy and his power (Luke 10:19). Because of His death and resurrection, Satan and his demons are under the feet of each believer, just as the Amorite kings were under the feet of the Israelites. Unless this spiritual fact is recognized, the enemy will wiggle his neck out of its vanquished position and try to exploit the believer who does not understand Satan's defeated position.

THE SOUTHERN CONQUEST (JOSH. 10:28–42)

Joshua and his army had chased the Amorites to Makkedah, and at this city the Israelites begin the next phase of their conquest. This section summarizes the campaign in southern Canaan. The list of victories over each city and its king may get a bit repetitious for us readers today. But for the Israelites each hard-fought victory brought them one step closer toward full occupation of the Promised Land. The conquest stretched south as far as Kadesh Barnea in the Negev and west to Gaza on the Mediterranean Sea. This dominion was achieved only because the Lord God was fighting for Israel. At the conclusion of the campaign the Israelites return to their base camp at Gilgal.

What was the fate of each city attacked by Joshua? (Josh. 10:28, 30, 32, etc.)

What was the fate of the kings of these cities? (Josh. 10:40)

 AT A GLANCE

From the following verses in chapter 10, name each of the seven cities destroyed in the southern conquest.

Verse 28

Verse 29

Verse 31

Verse 33

Verse 34

Verse 36

Verse 38

 FAITH ALIVE

What value would keeping a list of spiritual victories serve for you?

Would such a list be a helpful reminder of God's abundant blessings?

BEHIND THE SCENES

The country of Goshen mentioned in Joshua 10:41 should not be confused with the Goshen in Egypt, which comprised the northeastern region of the Nile delta. Jacob and his family settled in the latter when Joseph was prime minister of Egypt (Gen. 46:28). During the time of Moses, Goshen was spared the plagues that fell upon the rest of Egypt (Ex. 8:22; 9:26), and the Israelites abandoned their homes here when they made their exodus out of Egypt (Ex. 12:37).

The Goshen captured by Joshua was a district in southern Canaan that lay between Gaza and Gibeon, stretching southward through the hill country toward the Negev (Josh. 11:16). A town named Goshen is later mentioned in Joshua 15:51. Its site was in the southwest area of Judah, whose boundaries comprised much of the former country of Goshen.[2]

THE NORTHERN CONQUEST (JOSH. 11:1–15)

With the conquest of central and southern Canaan complete, Joshua was soon to face his most formidable opposition. Jabin, king of Hazor, organized a confederation of northern kings to repel the Israelites. Their massive army assembled at the waters of Merom to meet Israel's forces. Assured of victory by God, Joshua launched a surprise attack and totally routed the Canaanites, chasing them as far up the Mediterranean coast as Sidon. The Israelites totally destroyed each city as commanded by God, saving only the valuables and livestock as booty for themselves. Because Hazor was the head of the confederation, Joshua reserved a special punishment for this city. Of all the cities built on a mound, or tell, he burned only Hazor to the ground.

What five peoples comprised the northern Canaanite confederation? (Josh. 11:3)

How large was the Canaanite army that assembled at Merom? (Josh. 11:4)

What did Joshua do with the captured horses and chariots? (Josh. 11:9)

FAITH ALIVE

As we engage in spiritual warfare to gain God's promises, certain enemies, like Hazor, loom larger. They must be given special attention and dealt with more forcefully.

What is the major hindrance to receiving God's blessings now in your life?

What steps are you taking to remove that hindrance?

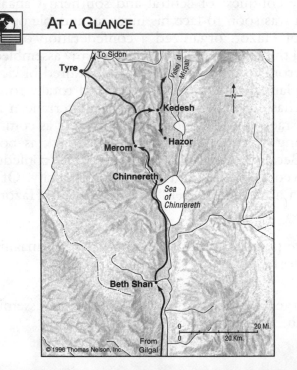

AT A GLANCE

🚪 BEHIND THE SCENES

Joshua's northern conquest circled the west side of the Sea of Chinneroth. Its eastern shore served as the border for the territory of Sihon, king of the Amorites (Josh. 12:3). This freshwater lake is thirteen miles long and eight miles at its widest. Its name—the Hebrew word for harp—is derived from its outline.[3] This harp-shaped body of water is better known by its New Testament name—the Sea of Galilee. Peter and Andrew lived along its northern shores in the town of Capernaum (Mark 1:29), which soon became the base for Jesus' Galilean ministry. Jesus did most of His miracles and gave most of His teaching on or around the Sea of Galilee.

The Gospels record two other names for the lake. The first is the Sea of Tiberias (John 6:1; 21:1), named for the large resort city on its western shore. Herod Antipas built the city in A.D. 20 as a political center for his kingdom.[4] The other name is the Lake of Gennesaret, derived from the fertile plain that lies above its northwestern shore (Josh. 11:2; Matt. 14:34). Chinneroth is mentioned again in Joshua 19:35, where it is named as one of the fortified cities in the land of Naphtali.

THE CONQUESTS OF MOSES AND JOSHUA (JOSH. 11:16—12:24)

With the victory in the northern campaign the Israelites had secured the land of Canaan promised to them by God. The four major regions were conquered—the Jordan Valley, the Judean hill country, the Negev, the Shephelah—as well as much of the Mediterranean coastal plain. Two mountains marked the other boundaries—Mount Halak in the south and Mount Hermon in the north. Only the Gibeonites had made peace with the Israelites; every other city was destroyed. Even the giants named Anakim were largely wiped out; only a remnant was left in the cities of Gaza, Gath, and Ashdod. Chapter 12 is a roll call of kings defeated by Moses and Joshua. Moses defeated the two kings who ruled east of the Jordan; Joshua defeated thirty-one kings who ruled in Canaan. The victory over all these kings signaled that God's covenant promises to Israel were indeed fulfilled.

What did God do to the Canaanites so that they would fight against Israel? (Josh. 11:20)

Where did the race of Anakim have their cities? (Josh. 11:21)

Who were the two kings that Moses defeated? (Josh. 12:2, 4)

Who were the first and last kings named in the list of thirty-one? (Josh. 12:9, 24)

 PROBING THE DEPTHS

Joshua 11:20 states that the Lord hardened the hearts of the Canaanites so that He might destroy them. Is God's character such that He denied these people their own free will? A similar situation is seen with Pharaoh. Exodus repeatedly states that God hardened Pharaoh's heart so that he would refuse to release the Israelites (Ex. 7:3, 13, 22; 9:12). As a result God brought ten plagues of judgment upon the Egyptians, including the final death plague upon the firstborn. The biblical answer to this question is best provided by Paul in Romans 1:18–32. He describes a type of people who deny the existence of God, in spite of the many evidences of His existence, and instead pursue stubbornly a lifestyle of idolatry and immorality. Because of their resistance to God, He then gives them up to debasing activities including homosexuality and other perversions. God hardens their hearts after they have first deadened themselves to the truth of His existence. The Canaanites were such a people, as we have seen, and God marked their civilization for destruction.

FAITH ALIVE

Occasionally we too can harden our hearts and become stubborn about doing God's revealed will. Such disobedience stops the flow of God's blessing in our lives and opens the door for Satan's activity.

Can you recall a time when you hardened your heart against God?

How did you reestablish a right relationship with God, and what was the result?

BEHIND THE SCENES

Who were these giants called the Anakim? They were descendants of Anak (Num. 13:33) and Arba (Num. 15:13), who themselves probably descended from the early race of giants called Nephilim (Gen. 6:4). Anakim means "long-necked people," and their great size caused the twelve spies to feel like grasshoppers in their sight (Num. 13:33). Although Joshua drove them out of the hill country, it was Caleb who expelled them from Hebron completely (Judg. 1:20). The Anakim found refuge in the Philistine cities of Gaza, Gath, and Ashdod (Josh. 11:22). Several centuries later the giant Goliath came from Gath to challenge the armies of Israel until David killed him with his sling (1 Sam. 17:4–51). This race of giants was finally exterminated in Judah's wars with the Philistines (1 Sam. 21:16–22).[5]

1. Donald H. Madvig, "Joshua," *Expositor's Bible Commentary*, Vol. 3 (Grand Rapids: Zondervan Publishing House, [1982]), 303–4.

2. *Nelson's New Illustrated Bible Dictionary* (Nashville: Thomas Nelson Publishers, 1995), 515–16, "Goshen."

3. Ibid., 473, "Galilee, Sea of."

4. Ibid., 1249–50, "Tiberias."

5. *Anchor Bible Dictionary*, Vol. 1 (New York: Doubleday, 1992), 222, "Anak."

Lesson 5/*Dividing God's Promise*
Joshua 13:1—21:45

One day the postman delivers a certified letter to your home, stating that your grandfather's estate will be distributed next week. Before his death, Grandpa Tony had promised that his properties in the country would be given to each of his grandchildren. When the day comes to go to the lawyer's office, are you going to stay home? Of course not! You want to know which piece of property you have inherited. After the reading of the will, you will want to see your inheritance as soon as possible. You will stop at the surveyor's office to get a plat of the land, showing the exact location. Then you'll walk around the property—climbing the hills, crossing the brook, and examining the trees. Your grandfather's promise has come to pass; this land is now yours!

Joshua 13 begins the second half of the book. Here the focus shifts from achieving God's promises to enjoying them. The land is divided among the tribes of Israel. These chapters make slow reading for us today because they are filled with unfamiliar geographical descriptions. But put yourself in the place of the Israelites, as the above story illustrates. What an exciting time it must have been for each tribe and family to finally possess the land promised to them in Canaan!

THE LAND PROMISED EAST OF THE JORDAN RIVER (JOSH. 13:1–33)

The description of Canaan's conquest in chapters 1—12 gives the impression that the Promised Land was solidly controlled by the Israelites. However, a somewhat different picture is presented by the time of Joshua's final years. For God tells

His servant that there is still land to be possessed. Yet Joshua is to divide all the land as if it were already his. Likewise, east of the Jordan several pockets remain to be conquered. This territory given by Moses is described first—the land given to Reuben, Gad, and the half tribe of Manasseh. The Levites share no part of the land either east or west of the Jordan, since their inheritance is the Lord God Himself.

What territory remains to be conquered west of the Jordan? (Josh. 13:2)

What territory remains to be conquered east of the Jordan? (Josh. 13:13)

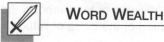

WORD WEALTH

Inheritance (Heb. *nachalah*) is a key word in Joshua, used fifty-seven times in the New King James Version. The fifty-one uses in chapters 13–21 highlight its special significance in this section. Canaan was Israel's special inheritance from God (Josh. 13:6). Each tribe received an inheritance by lot according to its population; then each family in the tribe was given its inheritance. These allotments were to remain in the family forever and could never be sold permanently. Hence in the Year of Jubilee any land lost through debt bondage was to be returned to its original owners (Lev. 25:10). To the Hebrews, the term "inheritance" had important spiritual and national associations that extended beyond the family property.[1]

FAITH ALIVE

Proverbs tells us that the godly leave an inheritance for their children and grandchildren (Prov. 13:22; 19:14). One of my greatest blessings was the modest inheritance left by my godly grandparents. The money provided the down payment for our family's first house. Economists tell us that in the next few years the largest transfer of wealth between generations in history will take place. If you will be receiving an inheritance in the future, what are your plans to be a good steward of it for your family and the kingdom of God?

What provisions are you making to bless your children and grandchildren with an inheritance?

AT A GLANCE

The following map shows the division of land among the twelve tribes as well as the designation of the cities of refuge.[2]

📖 BEHIND THE SCENES

Three major rivers flow into the Dead Sea and Jordan River from the east. These rivers played an important role in the division of the eastern lands. The southern boundary for Reuben's allotment was the Arnon River. The Jabbok River flowed through the center of Gad's allotment. Similarly the Yarmuk River flowed through the middle of Manasseh's allotment.

The land east of the Jordan called Gilead was especially suited for pasturing sheep and goats. Its principal city Heshbon lay in the territory of Reuben, just below the boundary with Gad. Jazer was a city in Gad's allotment that was particularly noted for its valuable grazing land. Manasseh's territory lay east of the Sea of Chinneroth and included the major business center of Ramoth Gilead. This city was the site of many battles, for whoever held it controlled the trade route between Syria and the King's Highway. With its water, pasture, and commercial viability, the land east of the Jordan had the potential to bring great prosperity to the tribes of Reuben, Gad, and Manasseh.

CALEB RECEIVES HIS PROMISE (JOSH. 14:1–15)

Whereas Moses had distributed the land east of the Jordan, Joshua was in charge of distributing the land west of the Jordan. This distribution was done by lot. Before the process could begin, one piece of unfinished business needed to be resolved. Caleb, the other faithful spy who had accompanied Joshua into Canaan, had yet to receive his inheritance promised by Moses. Even though he was not a young man, Caleb asked Joshua for a difficult prize. His target was the stronghold of the Anakim called Kirjath Arba. Mobilizing his fellow warriors of the tribe of Judah, he captured the mountain and renamed it Hebron. Caleb had finally received his promise of land in Canaan.

Who assisted Joshua in distributing the land? (Josh. 14:1)

How old was Caleb when Moses sent him to spy out Canaan, and how old was he now? (Josh. 14:7, 10)

What is stated about Caleb's physical condition? (Josh. 14:11)

FAITH ALIVE

What motivated Caleb to wait over forty years for his promise?

Can you recall a time when you gave a good report while the assessment of others was negative?

What attributes does Caleb possess that you wish to emulate?

BEHIND THE SCENES

The city of Hebron, situated nineteen miles southwest of Jerusalem, has a rich biblical history. For a long time Abraham made his home at Mamre in Hebron (Gen. 13:18). Here God made His covenant with Abraham, promising that he would be the father of many nations and that his descendants would inherit the land of Canaan (Gen. 17:1–9). At Hebron the Lord appeared to Abraham and Sarah and promised the birth of Isaac (Gen. 18:1–15). At her death Sarah was buried at Hebron in the cave of Machpelah (Gen. 23:19).

Hebron was likewise important in Judah's later history. David ruled from Hebron for seven years before making Jerusalem his capital (2 Sam. 2:11). Absalom used Hebron as his base when he fomented the rebellion against his father

David (2 Sam. 15:7–12). Rehoboam fortified the city because of its strategic role in protecting Judah's southern boundary (2 Chron. 11:10–12). Today Hebron is a center of contention in the Arab/Israeli conflict. Although the city sits in the occupied West Bank, Jewish settlers desire to live at Hebron because of its historical links to the patriarchs. The Arabs likewise claim Abraham as their father. Because of the volatile political situation, Hebron usually cannot be visited by tourists to Israel.

THE LAND PROMISED WEST OF THE JORDAN RIVER (JOSH. 15:1—19:51)

In the distribution of the land the first lot falls to tribe of Judah. Judah's allotment runs west of the Dead Sea to the Mediterranean Sea. A follow-up story concerning Caleb is related. He vows to give his daughter Achsah in marriage to the man who captures Kirjath Sepher. His nephew Othniel takes it, and thereby receives Achsah as his reward. The allotments for Ephraim and the rest of the tribe of Manasseh come next. They complain, however, that their portion is too small. Therefore Joshua promises them mountainous country belonging to the Perizzites as additional territory.

The assembly of Israel next moves to Shiloh accompanied by the ark of the covenant. Here the distribution to the seven remaining tribes takes place. First Joshua commissions these tribes to send three representatives each to survey the remaining land. After the survey is completed, Joshua casts lots before the Lord to make the distribution. Benjamin receives territory north of Judah while Simeon's territory actually falls within Judah's territory in the south which borders the Negev. Zebulun and Issachar both receive portions of the fertile Jezreel valley as their inheritance. Asher's allotment lies along the Mediterranean coast above Mount Carmel, while Naphtali's lies just to the east above the Sea of Chinneroth. Dan receives the final allotment—a small territory running from the Aijalon Valley to the Mediterranean coast at Gap. They also capture the city of Leshem in the upper Jordan valley, and rename it Dan. After every tribe receives its inheritance, Joshua receives a gift from the Israelites. They give him the city of Timnath in the mountains of Ephraim as his own personal inheritance.

What were the additional blessings that Achsah and Othniel received from Caleb? (Josh. 15:18–19)

Which Canaanite city refused to fall to the tribe of Ephraim? (Josh. 16:10)

 BEHIND THE SCENES

An unusual situation developed in the tribe of Manasseh concerning the estate of Zelophehad, who died in the wilderness. He had no sons, only five daughters. Since the inheritance customarily passed along to sons in a patriarchal society, the family would have no inheritance in the Promised Land. Therefore these five daughters boldly asked for their family possession from Moses. Their case was brought before the Lord, who affirmed their right to an inheritance (Num. 27:1–11). When Joshua made Manasseh's distribution in Canaan, Zelophehad's daughters stepped forward to claim their inheritance among their father's family (Josh. 17:4).

 FAITH ALIVE

The claim for equality by Zelophehad's daughters under the law is the first in the Bible. The Lord vindicates the petition of these women, establishing a precedent for similar cases in the future.

What attitudes do these five women display that caused them to win their case?

How does Moses respond in the face of this difficult problem?

BEHIND THE SCENES

Judah's northern boundary ran along the ridge above the Hinnom Valley, better known as Gehenna in the New Testament (Mark 9:43, 45, 47). Across the valley to the north and east lay the Jebusite city of Jebus (Josh. 15:8). Neither Joshua nor his warriors were ever successful in capturing this stronghold (Josh. 15:63). For several hundred years the Israelites were forced to coexist with the Jebusites.

That is, until King David came on the scene. This great warrior determined to take this seemingly impregnable fortress away from the Jebusites. Joab led the attack climbing up the city's water shaft and forcing a breach in the walls, which allowed David's warriors inside. Jebus now became known as Zion, the city of David (2 Sam. 5:6–9; 1 Chr. 11:4–7). David next united the tribes of Israel and Judah and moved his capital from Hebron to this city, which is best known as Jerusalem. He established Jerusalem not only as a political center but also as a religious one when he moved the ark of the covenant into the city (2 Sam. 6:12–19).

THE CITIES OF REFUGE AND OF THE LEVITES (JOSH. 20:1—21:45)

Two final allotments needed to be made. First, the Lord directed Joshua to designate six cities of refuge. Anyone who accidentally killed a person could flee to the safety of these cities without fear of retaliation. The cities of refuge were evenly distributed from north to south in the tribal territories, both east and west of the Jordan River. Second, although the Levites were not eligible for their own apportionment, each of the tribes was required to allot cities with outlying pasture lands for the priests. The tribe of Judah gave Kirjath Arba, the city taken by Caleb, to Aaron's descendants. Shechem—Jacob's city—was given to the Kohathites. Forty-eight cities were designated as Levitical cities and distributed among the twelve tribes of Israel. Each of the six cities of refuge was likewise a Levitical city. With these final distributions, God's promise of land to Israel was fulfilled. God gave the Israelites rest from their enemies as they now began to enjoy the fruits of this good land.

How long was the person who sought safety required to stay in a city of refuge? (Josh. 20:6)

Who gave the command to allot cities to the Levites? (Josh. 21:2)

Which family of Levites received the first allotment? (Josh. 21:10)

Which areas at Hebron did Caleb continue to keep? (Josh. 21:12)

BEHIND THE SCENES

The tribe of Levi was divided into three clans representing the sons of Levi—Gershon, Kohath, and Merari. The clan of Kohath was further divided into four families, one of which descended from Moses and Aaron. The Levites were not given land because God Himself was to be their portion (Num. 18:20). In addition to the sustenance received from their livestock, the Levites were eligible to receive a tithe from the people which was collected every three years (Deut. 26:12–13).

The Levitical cities were strategically located along the borders between the tribes. With six of the cities designated as cities of refuge, the Levites assumed an important judicial role among the people. They protected those who sought refuge until the elders of the city determined the guilt or innocence of the person. The Levitical cities became vital outposts for educating the Israelites about the Law. The Levites had a special teaching ministry among the twelve tribes (Deut. 33:8–10), and their dispersal throughout Israel allowed them to accomplish this mission. Three Levitical cities—Gibeon, Bethel, and Gilgal —later became important centers for Israel's political and spiritual life.[3]

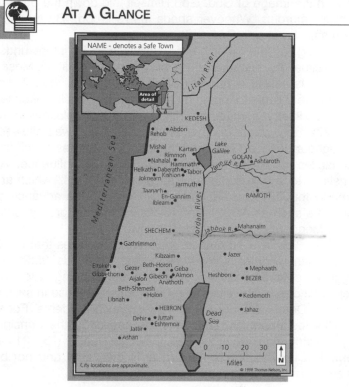

AT A GLANCE

THE LEVITICAL CITIES[4]

PROBING THE DEPTHS

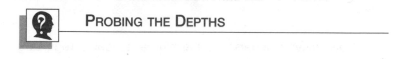

There is much discussion in society today about the pros and cons of capital punishment. The Bible is often brought into the discussion, especially the sixth commandment translated in the King James Version, "Thou shalt not kill" (Ex. 20:13). The New King James Version properly translates the original Hebrew meaning as "You shall not murder." The Bible clearly distinguishes between murder and killing. Murder is the deliberate and premeditated act of taking another person's life. Cain's slaying of Abel was the first murder in human history (Gen. 4:8). The reason for the seriousness of murder is that people are made in the image of God. God Himself laid down the punishment for murder: "Whoever sheds man's blood,/ By man his blood shall be shed" (Gen. 9:6).

Killing, on the other hand, is allowed in Scripture under certain situations because of the fallen human condition. Moses gave the Israelites a number of commandments that, if disobeyed, were liable for death by stoning. These capital offenses included idolatry, sorcery, and improper sexual relations (Lev. 20:1–27). Holy war is another area where killing was allowed. Throughout Joshua God commanded the Israelites to kill the Canaanites to purge the land of its heathen influence. As Christians today we sometimes speak of "just wars," which are primarily fought for self-defense or to restrain the advance of evil rulers such as Adolf Hitler. (Certain Christian groups such as the Mennonites are pacifists, however.)

The Bible is a pragmatic book and recognizes that involuntary manslaughter sometimes occurs. Leviticus 35:22–23 suggests several possible scenarios surrounding such an accidental death. The cities of refuge protected those in such a situation. Death was not the penalty for such incidents. For in the Old Testament all punishment is based on the principle of just retribution: "eye for eye, tooth for tooth" (Ex. 21:24; Deut. 19:21). The punishment must fit the crime and not be greater than the crime itself.

FAITH ALIVE

How do you understand the biblical teaching regarding war, murder, and killing?

If you were chosen to sit on a jury that was deciding a capital offense, could you vote for the death penalty based on the teaching of the Bible? If not, why couldn't you?

 ## BIBLE EXTRA

The theme of **rest** in the land is a prominent one in the Book of Joshua (Josh. 22:4). God promised Israel rest from the hardships of the wilderness (Josh. 1:13, 15), from the rigors of war (Josh. 11:23; 14:15), and from strife with her enemies (Josh. 21:44; 23:1). She was to be an example of a nation under God, witnessing to the peoples around her. Israel's rest was temporary because, as the Book of Judges shows, she disobeyed God's law and compromised with her neighbors. Israel was not to achieve rest in the land again until the time of David (2 Sam. 7:1). The northern kingdom was finally expelled from the land by the Assyrians in 722 B.C. and the southern kingdom by the Babylonians in 586 B.C. In the New Testament rest is one of the promises given to Christians. Jesus, the new Joshua, offered rest to all who come to Him (Matt. 11:28). The Book of Hebrews promises a rest for God's people, left unfulfilled by Joshua. This rest is achieved by ceasing from our human works and walking in faith, refusing to disobey God by hardening our hearts (Heb. 4:1–10).

FAITH ALIVE

Read Hebrews chapters 3—4 and define what the author means by rest.

Give several examples of how you have entered into God's rest.

1. *Nelson's New Illustrated Bible Dictionary* (Nashville: Thomas Nelson Publishers, 1995), 598, "Inheritance."

2. *Spirit-Filled Life® Bible* (Nashville: Thomas Nelson Publishers, 1991), 333, "Division of Land Among the Twelve Tribes and Designation of the Cities of Refuge."

3. *The Word in Life Study Bible* (Nashville: Thomas Nelson Publishers, 1996), 421–22, "The Levitical Cities."

4. Ibid., 421.

3.

4.

5.

 FAITH ALIVE

A popular tongue-in-cheek saying states, "Don't confuse me with the facts; I've already made up my mind." Can you recall a time when you made a decision about someone or something before all the facts were in?

What, if any, were the negative consequences of making such a hasty judgment?

What role do motives play in determining the guilt or innocence of someone's actions?

 WORD WEALTH

Two Hebrew words, *yerushah* and *'achuzzah*, stand behind the word translated **possession** in the Book of Joshua. The words are used interchangeably, with *yerushah* used in the early chapters (Josh. 1:15; 12:6, 7) and *'achuzzah* used exclusively in the final chapters (Josh. 21:12, 41; 22:4, 9, 19—two times). The language of possession in Joshua is closely tied to the covenantal promise of land given to Abraham

(Gen. 15:18–21; 17:8). Before the Israelites could possess Canaan, they first had to dispossess its inhabitants. Thus we see a link between God's promise and the people's response. God's promise was foundational, but to gain possession of the land the people had to risk their lives to receive it. Then to ensure continued possession the Israelites had to observe faithfully God's law (Deut. 4:5). Possession was therefore neither automatic nor irrevocable. The Israelite possession of Canaan required a combination of physical, moral, and religious strength.[1]

 PROBING THE DEPTHS

The Jordan River has served as a natural boundary throughout history, and in fact still serves as a border today. West of the river is Israel, east of it is Jordan. But what is meant by the term West Bank? Before the 1967 war in Palestine, Jordan's boundaries extended west of the Jordan River covering the biblical region called Samaria. In that war Israel pushed the Jordanian Army across the Jordan and claimed this territory west of the river as part of Israel. The towns in the region are settled largely by Arabs, and the Israeli government has recently given the Palestinians self-rule in this West Bank region. Mistrust and misunderstanding continue to characterize the relationship between the Arabs and Israelis living in this area today. Ongoing negotiations seek to diffuse the tension and violence between these two peoples of the Bible.

JOSHUA'S FAREWELL ADDRESS (JOSH. 23:1–16)

The Book of Joshua closes with two farewell speeches by Joshua. The first, recorded in chapter 23, is probably directed only to Israel's leaders; the second, discussed in the next section, is for all the people. At the close of Joshua's life Israel's leaders gather in Shiloh, the site of the altar and the resting place of the ark of the covenant. Joshua's recorded speech is probably a summary of a much longer address. He first reviews how each tribe received their allotment in the Promised Land. Then he issues specific warnings to these leaders about what will happen if they allow the Israelites to compromise with the Canaanites still in the land. If they promote obedience to God, it will result in His continued blessing. However, if they tolerate transgression, God's anger will bring destruction. How these men lead the nation in following God's commands will determine whether the Promised Land is a place of blessing or curse. Unlike the end of Deuteronomy, where Moses passes his mantle of leadership on to Joshua, Joshua designates no one to be his successor. The lack of a national leader will have dire consequences in the next generation.

What are the four groups of leaders whom Joshua addresses? (Josh. 23:2)

What practice with the Canaanites is specifically prohibited? (Josh. 23:13)

What four images describe how the Canaanites will act toward the Israelites if they no longer follow God? (Josh. 23:13)

 FAITH ALIVE

Why are godly leaders so important in leading a congregation to follow God's commandments?

What are the possible consequences if a church's leaders do not obey God's commands?

If you are a leader in your church, what are some specific ways that you can set a godly example before your small group or Sunday school class?

BIBLE EXTRA

Both Moses and Joshua gave farewell speeches at the close of their ministry. This is but one of many common experiences that the two shared. Find these similar experiences in the following chart.

Moses	Joshua	Similar Experience
Ex. 15:22	Josh. 4:19	
Ex. 12:21–28	Josh. 5:10–11	
Ex. 3:2–5	Josh. 5:13–15	
Deut. 9:25–29	Josh. 7:7–9	
Ex. 17:8–16	Josh. 8:26	
Ex. 17:15–16	Josh. 8:30	
Deut. 31–32	Josh. 23–24	
Deut. 34:5–7	Josh. 24:29–30	

FAITH ALIVE

What does the promise in Joshua 23:10 mean to you—that you can chase a thousand because the Lord fights for you?

What are some possible applications of this promise in your Christian life?

THE COVENANT AT SHECHEM (JOSH. 24:1–33)

The Books of Deuteronomy and Joshua have similar endings. Moses renews the covenant with the people in Moab before his death on Mount Nebo (Deut. 29:1; 34:5–7), while in this chapter Joshua renews the covenant with the people at Shechem before his death on Mount Gaash. Joshua opens his address with a survey of redemption history beginning with Abraham, who was the first to visit Canaan. Like Moses, Joshua reviews Israel's struggle after the Exodus, first, to win the territory east of the Jordan and, second, to conquer Canaan after crossing over the river. He then challenges the Israelites to choose God and forsake idolatry. That is the decision he and his household have already made. The people respond, vowing they will never forsake God and follow foreign gods. This exchange between Joshua and the people occurs two more times, providing a threefold witness to their commitment to serve the Lord. Joshua erects a stone near the sanctuary to serve as a witness to the covenant made at Shechem that day. Each family then departs to its inheritance in the Promised Land. Shortly after, Joshua dies at the age of 110, ten years short of that of his mentor Moses.

What was unique about the land, cities, vineyards, and olive groves that the Israelites received? (Josh. 24:13)

What had Joshua and his family chosen regarding the God

of Israel? (Josh. 24:15)

What did Joshua do with the words of his speech? (Josh. 24:26)

What other important Israelite died about this time? (Josh. 24:33)

BEHIND THE SCENES

Making a covenant (Heb. *berith*), or treaty, was a common practice in the ancient world of the Bible.[2] Such archaeological discoveries as the Mari documents and the Amarna tablets record treaties made by neighbors of Israel. A vassal treaty—the type that God made with the Israelites and that Israel made with Gibeon—was made between a greater and a lesser power. Such a treaty typically had five elements:

1. Preamble stating the names and titles of the parties

2. Historical introduction describing the previous relations of the parties

3. Stipulation of responsibilities of both parties

4. List of divine witnesses

5. Statement of curses and blessings.

All the covenants in the Old Testament, both divine and human, usually have these elements represented in one form or another.

At the Last Supper Jesus instituted the new covenant with His disciples. Read Luke 22:14–22 and note the common features with the five elements of a Near Eastern covenant just mentioned.

FAITH ALIVE

In Joshua 24:19 the Lord is called a holy and a jealous God. In what ways is He a holy God?

In what ways is He a jealous God?

AT A GLANCE[3]

THE PEOPLES OF THE OLD TESTAMENT

Joshua mentioned seven tribes that the Israelites found living in Canaan at the time of the conquest (Josh. 24:11). The table below summarizes who these groups were.

Name	Description
Amorites (Gen. 15:16)	A nomadic, barbarous people living in Canaan at the time of Abraham.
Canaanites (Josh. 3:10)	The dominant civilization of Canaan between the twenty-first and sixteenth centuries B.C., expelled by the Israelites.
Girgashites	Descendants of Canaan frequently listed among Canaanite tribes.
Hittites	Descendants of Heth, the son of Canaan, they lived in the Judean hills near Hebron (probably not related to the Hittite empire of Syria).
Hivites	Descendants of Canaan, they lived in Lebanon into the time of Solomon, who conscripted them into his labor force (1 Kin. 9:20).
Jebusites	Descendants of Canaan and inhabitants of Jebus (Jerusalem), which was captured by David (2 Sam.5:6–7).
Perizzites	An obscure tribe frequently mentioned with the Canaanite tribes, their name may mean "villagers"; seem to have preferred to live among the hills of Canaan.

BIBLE EXTRA

Before Joseph died in Egypt, he made his relatives vow that they would bury him in the land promised to Abraham, Isaac, and Jacob. Following his death, Joseph's body was embalmed as a mummy according to Egyptian burial practices (Gen. 50:24–26). When the Israelites left Egypt in the Exodus, Moses made a point of carrying Joseph's bones with them in fulfillment of their oath (Ex. 13:19). The final chapter of this episode fittingly concludes the Book of Joshua. Joseph's bones are buried in Shechem at the plot of ground purchased by Jacob and now the inheritance of Joseph's children (Josh. 24:32). Joseph had come home!

FAITH ALIVE

The Bible says that honoring our father and mother is the first commandment with a promise: "that it may be well with you and you may live long on the earth" (Eph. 6:2–3; see Ex. 20:12).

What are some ways in which you are honoring your father and mother?

Have you made any promises to your parents or grandparents regarding their future care? Are you fulfilling these promises?

BEHIND THE SCENES

Shechem is a very important city in the Bible. Its name, meaning "shoulder," probably comes from its location on the slope, or shoulder, of Mount Ebal. Abraham made his first camp in Canaan here at the terebinth tree of Moreh. After God promised to give this land to his descendants, Abraham built an altar here (Gen. 12:6–7). Jacob also stopped at Shechem and bought a parcel of land from Hamor. On this land he also erected an altar called El Elohe Israel (Gen. 33:18–20). Shechem was the home of Gideon's son Abimelech (Judg. 9:1). At Shechem, Rehoboam was rejected as Solomon's successor to rule the united monarchy and instead became king only of Judah (1 Kin. 12:1–19). Jereboam became king of Israel and made Shechem the first capital of the northern kingdom (1 Kin. 12:25). In the time of Jesus, Shechem was the chief city of the Samaritans. Nearby at Sychar, Jesus had his important meeting with the Samaritan woman at Jacob's well (John 4:5).

  AT A GLANCE[4]

The TRUTH-IN-ACTION through JOSHUA		
Letting the LIFE of the Holy Spirit Bring Faith's Works Alive in You!		
Truth Joshua Teaches	Text	**Action** Joshua Invites
1 **Keys to Knowing God and His Ways** Joshua shows much about how God responds to godly lives. Prov. 16:7 says, "When a man's ways please the LORD, He makes even his enemies to be at peace with him." Joshua reveals many benefits of knowing the ways of God with men whose ways please Him.	2:8–11, 24; 3:7 4:19–24 21:45; 23:14	**Expect** God's favor when you follow His Word and the Spirit's direction and when your ways please Him. **Know** that you will encounter no obstacle God cannot work in and through you to overcome. **Rest** in the confidence that God will never fail to fulfill His promises to you when your ways please Him.
2 **Steps to Dynamic Devotion** Joshua continues to call God's people to devote themselves completely to the Lord. In a day when so many follow the Lord with only partial devotion, Joshua and Caleb, "who wholly followed the LORD," provide challenging examples of the life the Lord honors.	9:14 14:18, 9, 14 22:5; 23:6	**Seek** the Lord prayerfully for every decision you make. **Know** that you cannot consistently make good decisions without His Word and Spirit. **Follow** God wholeheartedly and be devoted to Him. Doing so will yield a rich inheritance. **Be careful** faithfully to apply all of God's Word to all of your life. **Follow** Him with all of your heart and soul.
3 **Steps to Holiness** Joshua continually exhorts God's people to live holy lives. God's holy people will live *unto* Him and *apart from* the world. Joshua demonstrates that our failure to live in holiness can and will have dire consequences.	6:18, 19 23:7 24:23	**Do not covet** this world's goods. **Understand** that things we strive to get for ourselves will seriously weaken our walk with God. **Be careful** to not adopt this world's way of thinking and behavior. **Hold fast,** rather, to God's ways and serve Him wholeheartedly. **Reject** and **turn away** from this world and its ways. **Be assured** that you will thus be free to fully yield your heart to God.

The TRUTH-IN-ACTION through JOSHUA
Letting the LIFE of the Holy Spirit Bring Faith's Works Alive in You!

Truth Joshua Teaches	Text	Action Joshua Invites
4 Guidelines for Growing in Godliness Growing in godliness through knowing and applying God's Word is a recurring theme in Joshua. Simply knowing God's Word is not enough. We must know God's Word well enough to apply it to life's situations. God's promises that this kind of faithfulness to His Word will result in a successful and prosperous life.	1:7, 8 4:4–7 5:2–9 8:34, 35	**Practice regularly** Scripture memorization and meditation. Then **determine beforehand** to put it into practice. This promises sure success. **Establish memorials** in your spiritual journey. **Keep a record** of your experiences with God. **Share** these to instruct and encourage others. As God's people were circumcised for a sign, **be baptized. Rehearse** baptism's meaning and benefits (Col. 2:11–15). **Know** that this is a key to spiritual victory. **Incorpoate** regular Scripture reading as a part of personal and corporate worship.
5 Keys to Wise Living Good theology must always impact the way we live. Knowing God's Word but not knowing how to apply it is foolish and futile. Joshua helps us apply faithfully what we know about God's Word.	1:6, 7, 9 15:63; 16:10; 17:12	**Rely** on God's strength and wisdom, not your own. **Allow** God's abiding presence to give you courage: **Know** that Jesus' promise to be ever with you will keep you from terror and discouragement. **Do not rely** on your own strength and wisdom when dealing with sin. **Be assured** that without God you will have no success.
6 Steps to Dealing with Sin The failure to detect and deal with sin caused Israel's defeat at Ai. Past successes can cause us to be less careful about sin. None of us can afford to drop our guard, for even one person's sins can weaken the life of a whole church.	7:10–13 11:11	**Understand** that individual sin weakens the whole church. **Deal with sin** quickly and forthrightly. **Leave** no sin unconfessed or undealt with. **Be aware** that unconfessed sin will become a snare.
7 Guidelines to Gaining Victory Joshua is a type of Christ who always leads His people in victory and triumph. Our victories result from surrendering to Jesus' lordship and allowing Him to work through us to overcome our obstacles and adversities.	5:14, 15 17:18	**Submit yourself** continually to Jesus' lordship in your life. **Acknowledge** that He comes as the Captain of His army to lead us to victory (see Ex. 17:14, 15). **Be assured** that regardless of the strength of the enemy, God can and will enable you to prevail.

1. *International Standard Bible Encyclopedia,* Vol. 3 (Grand Rapids: Eerdmans Publishing Company, 1986), 910–11, "Possess, Possession."

2. *International Standard Bible Encyclopedia,* Vol. 1 (Grand Rapids: Eerdmans Publishing Company, 1979), 790, "Covenant (OT)."

3. Adapted from *Word in Life Study Bible* (Nashville: Thomas Nelson Publishers, 1996), 428–29, "The Peoples of the Old Testament."

4. *Spirit-Filled Life® Bible* (Nashville: Thomas Nelson Publishers, 1991), 341–42, "Truth-in-Action through Joshua."

Lesson 7/Testing Regarding God's Promise
Judges 1:1—3:31

The marshal's badge and six-gun always stood for what was right. Each week when I was growing up, Marshal Matt Dillon and his deputy Chester cleaned up the bad guys around Dodge City, Kansas, on the popular television show, "Gunsmoke." This and the other TV westerns of that time were in fact morality plays. You always knew who the bad guys were (they usually wore black), and the good guys, in spite of adversity, always won.

If there is a biblical equivalent to the Wild West, it is the period of the Book of Judges. The narrative style of Judges is much like Joshua, with its depictions of human nature being frank and occasionally brutal. If made into a movie, some of the scenes it describes would be R-rated! Judges is the focus for the second half of our study. Its theme is *restoring the promise of God.* The possession of the Promised Land, so triumphantly depicted in Joshua, is compromised by subsequent generations through idolatry and disobedience. In spite of Israel's apostasy, a gracious and loving God intervenes repeatedly to restore His people to their precious inheritance. Get ready for a roller-coaster ride as we work our way through the Book of Judges!

At A Glance[1]

FOCUS	DETERIORATION		DELIVERANCE						DEPRAVITY		
REFERENCE	1:1——————2:1——3:5		——4:1——6:1——10:6————			12:8——13:1——		17:1——19:1—20:1—21:25				
DIVISION	ISRAEL FAILS TO COMPLETE THE CONQUEST	GOD JUDGES ISRAEL	SOUTHERN CAMPAIGN	NORTHERN CAMPAIGN (1st)	CENTRAL CAMPAIGN	EASTERN CAMPAIGN	NORTHERN CAMPAIGN (2nd)	WESTERN CAMPAIGN	SIN OF IDOLATRY	SIN OF IMMORALITY	SIN OF CIVIL WAR
TOPIC	CAUSES OF THE CYCLES		CURSE OF THE CYCLES						CONDITIONS DURING THE CYCLES		
	LIVING WITH THE CANAANITES		WAR WITH THE CANAANITES						LIVING LIKE THE CANAANITES		
LOCATION	CANAAN										
TIME	c. 350 YEARS										

Nelson's Complete Book of Bible Maps and Charts © 1993 by Thomas Nelson, Inc.

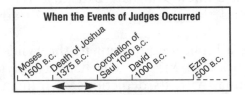

When the Events of Judges Occurred

Moses 1500 B.C.   Death of Joshua 1375 B.C.   Coronation of Saul 1050 B.C.   David 1000 B.C.   Ezra 500 B.C.

 ## Behind the Scenes

The Book of Judges is the second book of the Former Prophets, and, like Joshua, its author is unknown. The recurring statement, "In those days there was no king in Israel" (Judg. 17:6; 18:1; 19:1; 21:25), suggests a date after the period of the Judges, perhaps during the early monarchy under Saul or David around 1000 B.C. The Talmud ascribes its authorship to Samuel, so it is indeed possible that this prophet or a contemporary of his was the author. Certain parts of the book come from earlier sources. Deborah's song in chapter 5 was probably written by her. Jotham's fable of the trees (Judg. 9:8–15) uses the form of a traditional folktale. And Samson's riddles (Judg. 14:14, 18; 15:16) were certainly composed by this judge. The author of Judges has utilized these and other sources to give us a disturbing yet hopeful account of Israel during this difficult transitional period of her history.

Name the reminders of the period of the Judges that are still evident in the author's day.

Judges 1:21

Judges 1:26

Judges 6:24

Judges 10:4

Judges 15:19

Judges 18:12

Continuing Conquest of the Promised Land (Judg. 1:1–36)

The beginning of the Book of Judges is somewhat repetitive. The death of Joshua is mentioned twice (1:1; 2:7–10). It repeats the story, first recounted in Joshua 15:13–19, of Othniel capturing Kirjath Sepher (Judg. 1:11–15). This is undoubtedly because Othniel is mentioned as the first judge in chapter 3. There are also some confusing elements. First, the tribe of Judah is said to have captured Jerusalem (1:8), then the tribe of Benjamin is said to have failed to capture Jerusalem (1:21). Also, the conquest of Canaan seems nearly complete in the opening verses (1:1–26); later, the conquest is presented as incomplete (1:27–36). This same tension, of course, appears in the Book of Joshua. The completion of the conquest of Canaan depends on the people's obedience to God.

Which tribe was the first to go up against the Canaanites? (Judg. 1:1)

Why did the captured king Adoni-Bezek have his thumbs and big toes cut off? (Judg. 1:6–7)

Where did Moses' Kenite relatives decide to settle? (Judg. 1:16)

How did the Israelites capture the city of Bethel, formerly called Luz? (Judg. 1:23–25)

Where did the Amorites force the children of Dan to live? (Judg. 1:34)

FAITH ALIVE

The tribe of Judah was chosen to go up first to take the land promised by God (Judg. 1:2). Their enthusiasm to follow God's call and to cooperate with their brothers from Simeon is shown in their response to the challenge, "Come up with me to my allotted territory, that we may fight against the Canaanites" (Judg. 1:3).

When an opportunity to serve God is presented, are you among the first or the last people to respond?

How might you better imitate the "Judah spirit" by acting boldly to take your own spiritual inheritance promised by God?

When obstacles arise in pursuing God's promises, do you tend to give up or do you press on toward the prize?

ISRAEL'S DISOBEDIENCE AND UNFAITHFULNESS (JUDG. 2:1—3:6)

The Angel of the Lord comes up to Bochim, the place of weeping, to deliver His solemn warning. Although God will never break his covenant with Israel, the nation has disobeyed Him by making a covenant with the Canaanites. Because of her disobedience, God will not drive Israel's enemies out of Canaan but will leave them to buffet the people. Joshua's death is truly the nail in the coffin signaling the transition to the next unfaithful generation. Yet, in spite of God's anger against Israel's spiritual harlotry, when the people cry out to God, He sends deliverers called judges to rescue them. However, such deliverance is only temporary and Israel's inclination toward unfaithfulness returns again and again.

To what two things are the Canaanites who remain in the land compared? (Judg. 2:3)

Where was Joshua buried after his death? (Judg. 2:9)

When did the Israelites usually revert to following other gods? (Judg. 2:19)

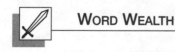

WORD WEALTH

The Hebrew word for **judges,** *shophetim,* is derived from the verb *shaphat,* which means "to judge," "decide," and "pronounce sentence."[2] Our concept of judges is one of individuals who preside over some legal judgment in a court of law. Because of such an association, we are apt to get an incorrect picture of the judges of Israel. These judges were raised up by God to function more as military leaders than civil officials. Their job was to deliver Israel from the foreign nations that oppressed them. Often they possessed little leadership experience (Gideon) or their behavior led their own countrymen to disavow them (Samson). Only Deborah functioned as a judge in the more conventional sense by issuing judgments to the people under the palm tree in Ephraim (Judg. 4:5). God Himself is called the divine Judge who renders judgment between the Israelites and their enemies (Judg. 11:27).

 ## FAITH ALIVE

One reason that God left enemies in the land was to test the subsequent generations who had never experienced war. Having to confront their enemies firsthand would give the Israelites personal experience of battle (Judg. 3:1–2). God likewise deals with us when He forgives our sins. We are delivered from certain sins instantly at salvation; other sins must be dealt with on an ongoing basis.

What particular sins/addictions/behaviors were you freed from at salvation?

What other sins seem to beset and ensnare you on an ongoing basis?

If you have already experienced victory over a certain problem of your life, how did God lead you to overcome it?

If you are presently struggling in a particular area, list four action steps you can take to have spiritual victory over these weaknesses of the flesh. For example, if lust is a problem, what

stores, magazines, movies, etc. do you need to avoid? If glut-
tony, what restaurants, grocery aisles, foods, etc. do you need
to forgo?

1.

2.

3.

4.

BEHIND THE SCENES

The period of the judges is presented throughout the book
as a cyclical pattern of sin-oppression-deliverance. It could
better be termed a downward spiral because each "cycle"
depicts a deterioration not only in the quality of the judge but
also in the effectiveness of his or her leadership. This pattern,
emphasized through the use of repeated language, is as follows:
1. The people of Israel "do evil" through idolatry and inter-
   marriage (2:11; 3:7, 12; 4:1; 6:1; 10:6; 13:1).
2. God sends a nation to oppress them (2:14; 3:8; 4:2;
   10:9).
3. In their oppression the people cry out to God (3:9, 15;
   6:6 7; 10:10).
4. God hears their cry and raises up a judge as their deliverer (2:16; 3:9, 15; 10:1, 12).

5. The oppressor is defeated and a time of rest follows under the leadership of a judge who finally dies (3:10–11; 8:28–32; 10:1–5; 12:9–15).

Although not every detail is mentioned in each "cycle," this pattern is largely followed throughout the Book of Judges.[3]

 ## BIBLE EXTRA

The Angel of the Lord who comes up from Gilgal to Bochim (Judg. 2:1) is a mysterious messenger who appears several times in the Old Testament. When Hagar, pregnant with Ishmael, fled into the wilderness following Sarah's reproof, the Angel located Hagar and gave her a promise regarding her child. Hagar calls the Angel "the God who sees" (Gen. 16:6–13). When Moses was in the desert, the Angel appeared to him in the burning bush. He identifies Himself "I AM WHO I AM," the God of Abraham, Isaac, and Jacob (Ex. 3:2–15). Later God promises to send His Angel before the Israelites when they battle the Canaanites for the Promised Land (Ex. 23:20–23). This Angel is undoubtedly the Commander whom Joshua meets on the plains of Jericho (Josh. 5:13–15). The Angel later appears to Gideon in Ophrah and announces that he will be the savior of Israel (Judg. 6:11–24). The Angel also appears to Manoah and his wife to announce the birth of Samson (Judg. 13: 3–23). Although humans were not allowed to see the face of God, the Angel could have contact with people (Ex. 33:20). The Angel thus appears as a divine figure, but still is spoken of as distinct from God (2 Sam. 24:16; Zech. 1:12). It seems best to understand the Angel of the Lord as the second person of the Trinity, Jesus Christ, before His incarnation.[4]

If this Angel really is Jesus, why do you think He is identified as the Angel of the Lord in the Old Testament?

For what reason(s) do you think the Angel appears to various people in the Old Testament?

THE FIRST JUDGES (JUDG. 3:7–31)

Because of Israel's worship of idols, God delivered the nation to Cushan-Rishathaim, king of Mesopotamia, for eight years. In response to the Israelites' plea for deliverance, God raises up the first judge, Othniel, nephew of Caleb. Othniel had already distinguished himself as a warrior by taking the Anakim stronghold of Kirjath Sepher (Judg. 1:12–13). When the Spirit of the Lord comes upon him, he prevails over the Mesopotamian army, giving Israel a forty-year rest. Then God raises up the Moabites, Ammonites, and Amalekites against Israel. The Israelites spend eighteen years in servitude to King Eglon before God raises up a left-handed Benjamite named Ehud. Ehud cunningly plans the assassination of Eglon and stabs the king to death in his own inner chamber. In the ensuing confusion Ehud escapes and rallies Israel against the Moabites. Ten thousand enemies are killed, and the land rests for eighty years. A final judge named Shamgar is mentioned who delivers Israel from the Philistines. Three different enemies, three different judges, but the same God fulfills His promise of rest in Canaan once His people repent and forsake their spiritual harlotry.

Which particular Canaanite gods did the Israelites serve? (Judg. 3:7)

Why was Ehud allowed access to King Eglon? (Judg. 3:17–18)

With what weapon did Shamgar kill the Philistines? (Judg. 3:31)

 **AT A GLANCE**

The judges of Israel arose from various tribes and from various regions of the country. The following map shows the geographical background of the judges of Israel.[5]

BEHIND THE SCENES

The Holy Spirit plays a prominent role in the Book of Judges. Deborah spoke as a prophetess under the anointing of the Holy Spirit (Judg. 4:4) as did another unnamed prophet (Judg. 6:8). The Holy Spirit came upon Othniel (3:10), Gideon (6:34), Jephthah (11:29), and Samson (13:24; 14:6, 19). These judges received a special enduement of power that enabled them to fulfill their calling.

Was their experience of the Spirit different from ours today? The Holy Spirit, because He is divine like Jesus, is the same yesterday, today, and forever. He is truly the Spirit of power and holiness. He acts on behalf of the people of God, whether they are Israel or the church. The miracles in Judges are consistent with those seen in the Book of Acts, although their operation and purposes are different. When the Holy Spirit came upon the judges, it was occasional and temporary, whereas in the New Testament the Spirit's coming is a permanent indwelling. Therefore, in addition to the Spirit's power, the fruit of the Spirit can develop, a deficiency clearly seen in Jephthah and Gideon. Today the gift of the Holy Spirit is our great inheritance, promised to us, our children, and future generations who believe (Acts 2:38–39).

Have you been filled with the Holy Spirit and when?

Describe how you have changed since the Holy Spirit came upon you in power and holiness.

Read the list of the fruit of the Spirit in Galatians 5:22–23. Which of these fruit is God now developing in your life?

AT A GLANCE[6]

THE TWELVE JUDGES OF ISRAEL		
Judge	Duration of Leadership	Major Accomplishments
Othniel (3:7–11)	40 years	Caleb's nephew; defeated a king of Mesopotamia.
Ehud (3:12–30)	80 years	Left-handed; killed Eglon, king of Moab, and subdued the Moabites.
Shamgar	Unknown	Killed 600 Philistines.
Deborah (4:4–5:31)	40 years	Recruited Barak to lead Israelite warriors to victory over a Canaanite king, Jabin, and his general, Sisera.
Gideon (6:11–8:32)	40 years	With an "army" of only 300, defeated the Midianites.
Tola (10:1–2)	23 years	Unknown.
Jair (10:3–5)	22 years	Unknown.
Jephthah (11:1–12:7)	6 years	Subdued the Ammonites, but at the cost of his daughter whom he vowed to sacrifice as a burnt offering; disciplined the Ephraimites.
Ibzan (12:8–10)	7 years	Unknown.
Elon (12:11–12)	10 years	Unknown.
Abdon (12:13–15)	8 years	Unknown.
Samson (13:2–16:31)	20 years	Harassed the Philistines; destroyed a pagan temple and killed many at the cost of his own life.

1. *Nelson's Complete Book of Bible Maps & Charts* (Nashville: Thomas Nelson Publishers, 1996), 75, "Judges at a Glance," "When the Events in Judges Occurred."

2. *Spirit-Filled Life® Bible* (Nashville: Thomas Nelson Publishers, 1991), 349, "Word Wealth: 2:18, judge."

3. Raymond B. Dillard and Tremper Longman III, *An Introduction to the Old Testament* (Grand Rapids: Zondervan Publishing House, 1994), 124–25.

4. *Nelson's New Illustrated Bible Dictionary* (Nashville: Thomas Nelson Publishers, 1995), 56, "Angel of God, Angel of the Lord."

5. *Spirit-Filled Life® Bible*, 349, "The Judges of Israel."

6. Adapted from *Word in Life Study Bible* (Nashville: Thomas Nelson Publishers, 1996), 439, "The Lord Raised Up Judges."

Lesson 8/Overcoming Prejudice in Realizing God's Promise
Judges 4:1—5:31

The ringing of bells at sidewalk kettles seems to herald the advent of the Christmas season each year. The Salvation Army is renowned for its ministry to the poor and needy, yet few of us know the dramatic story of its cofounder, Catherine Booth.

Her husband William was an English Methodist minister when she received her own call to ministry. Soon she was sharing the pulpit with her husband, and after he became ill, Catherine took over his entire preaching circuit. In 1865 the couple moved to West London, where Catherine did revivalistic preaching as well as city mission work. The couple founded the Salvation Army in 1875, with a major focus on reclaiming poorer women from a life of prostitution.

Women always have had significant leadership roles in the Salvation Army. In 1880 a team of seven women came over to establish the Army in the United States, but they encountered fierce opposition. In 1882 some six hundred assaults were reported against Army volunteers. One-third of these victims were women, including one who died of her wounds. The courage of the Army's women prompted William Booth to declare, "My best men are women."

Catherine's final years were devoted to preaching and rescue-mission work, especially among teenage prostitutes. She died of cancer in 1890 at the age of sixty-one. The legacy of this

Christian woman who overcame prejudice and opposition lives on today in the Salvation Army.[1]

Although female leaders are seldom mentioned in the Old Testament, in this lesson we will look at an anointed woman of faith who led Israel to a mighty deliverance from her enemies.

THE VICTORY OF DEBORAH (JUDG. 4:1–16)

Although Hazor had been destroyed by Joshua (Josh. 11:11), a weakened Israel allows the city to be rebuilt. Under King Jabin the Canaanites now rule the Israelites. During this period the prophetess Deborah (meaning "Bee"), wife of Lapidoth, begins to judge Israel in Ephraim. Through her God gives a prophetic word that the Israelites should mobilize ten thousand men to fight Sisera, the commander of Jabin's army. The Israelite commander Barak refuses to lead unless Deborah accompanies him. Because of his hesitation to act on the word of the Lord given through Deborah, Barak loses his share of the glory in the coming victory. In the battle the Israelites destroy the Canaanites and their chariots.

With how many iron chariots did Jabin oppress the Israelites? (Judg. 4:3, 13)

How did the Israelites respond to a female judge? (Judg. 4:5)

Which two tribes were mobilized against Jabin? (Judg. 4:6)

Where were Barak's troops gathered for the battle? (Judg. 4:12, 14)

FAITH ALIVE

Sometimes our hesitation in obeying God causes us to

lose out on some of His blessings. This is what happened in Barak's case. Why do you think Barak hesitated in obeying Deborah's command?

Can you name a situation when your hesitation to obey God has cost you a blessing?

In the faith hall of fame in Hebrews 11, why do you think the writer included Barak (v. 32) but omitted Deborah?

BEHIND THE SCENES

The royal dynasty of Jabin that reigned in Hazor posed an ongoing problem for the Israelites. In Joshua's day Jabin led the northern confederation of kings that opposed the Israelite conquest (Josh. 11:1, 10). For his role this Jabin was killed at Hazor's destruction. A later Jabin again oppressed the Israelites during the period of the judges.

Hazor was strategically located ten miles north of the Sea of Chinneroth and situated on a mound that dominated the Huleh Plain below. The site was first occupied in the third millennium B.C. Although many of the northern Canaanite cities were built on a mound (Heb. *tel* or Arab. *tell*), only Hazor was burned by Joshua. A tell is formed when a city is destroyed and the rubble subsequently leveled when a new city is built on the site. Over the centuries the mound grows higher and higher. Archaeologists use tells to identify ancient city sites and then begin their excavations on the top. By digging down through the various levels, they can date the strata by using the pottery and other artifacts that are found. Hazor, with its upper and lower city, is one of the largest archaeological sites in Israel. When Israeli archaeologist Yigael Yadin excavated Hazor, called Tell el-Qedah today, he discovered evidence of large-scale destruction dating to the 13th century B.C. While this finding is consistent with the projected late date for the Israelite conquest (about 1250 B.C.), the archaeological data seems to pose problems for an early date (about 1400 B.C.) for the conquest. Hazor proved to be a major Canaanite stronghold in northern Israel.[2]

BIBLE EXTRA

Women were used many times by God in the Old Testament, going beyond their traditional roles in male-dominated ancient society. From the following passages, identify the woman and her God-given task.

• Genesis 21:1–7

• Exodus 2:1–10

• Exodus 15:20–21

• Joshua 2:1–21

• 1 Samuel 1:8—2:10

• 1 Kings 1:11–40

• 2 Kings 22:14–20

• Esther 8:1–17

❓ PROBING THE DEPTHS

Women in ministry is presently a very controversial topic in the church. While some evangelical denominations allow women to be involved in public ministry, others prohibit the practice, basing their decision on such texts as 1 Timothy 2:12. Pentecostals and charismatics bring a unique perspective to the issue based on theological and historical considerations. When God poured out His Spirit on the Day of Pentecost, that outpouring was for men **and** women. Both could prophesy and speak in tongues (Acts 2:17–18). Faith in Jesus and water baptism validates that there is neither male nor female in Christ; all are Abraham's seed and heirs of God's promise (Gal. 3:28–29). The gifts of the Holy Spirit are given both to men and women for the benefit of all (1 Cor. 12:7–11). This is especially true in the church meeting where all must participate for mutual edification (1 Cor. 14:1–32).

Historically, women were very influential in the early Pentecostal movement. On the evening of January 1, 1901, Agnes C. Ozmun was the first person in this century to receive the baptism of the Holy Spirit accompanied by speaking in tongues. Her experience while a student at Charles Parham's Bethel Bible Institute helped launch this movement. Aimee Semple McPherson was the founder of the International Church of the Foursquare Gospel. And countless other women planted churches and served as missionaries as Pentecostalism spread around the world. Without the contribution of women the Pentecostal/charismatic movement would not have grown to be the largest theological stream within Protestantism today.

If you are a woman, what unique gifts has the Lord given you to bless and equip the body of Christ? How are you using these gifts?

If you are a man, how might you help your wife or a female friend release her gifts for the service of others?

Can women minister in your local church? Do you agree or disagree?

What is your point of view regarding women in leadership positions, and how do you support it from the Word of God?

BEHIND THE SCENES

One military advantage that the Canaanites had over the Israelites was that they possessed iron chariots (Josh. 17:16, 18; Judg. 1:19; 4:3, 13). Archaeologists date civilizations in the Middle East by the predominant metal in use. The Late Bronze Age (1550–1200 B.C.) was characterized by the use of bronze, an alloy of copper and tin. This is the period of Moses' Exodus and Joshua's conquest. The Early Iron Age (1200–900 B.C.) brought the introduction of iron tools. Although the Egyptians and the Hittites of Asia Minor used iron at an earlier period, it was the Philistines who learned the secret of smelting iron around 1200 B.C. This gave the Philistines the upper hand in their battles with the Israelites. Later, when the Philistines controlled Israel, they prohibited the Israelites from using iron, even for tools (1 Sam. 13:19, 22). Iron chariots were a formidable obstacle, but even one that the God of Israel could overcome, as Deborah and Barak's victory testifies.[3]

JAEL'S VICTORY (JUDG. 4:17–24)

Barak's hesitation to listen to Deborah causes the glory of victory to be given to a woman. Following the Israelite rout, Sisera flees and seeks refuge with Jael, the wife of Heber the Kenite, who was a relative of Moses. Jael welcomes Sisera to her tent, provides him a blanket, and then gives him milk to drink. While Sisera falls asleep from exhaustion, Jael kills the Canaanite commander. For a woman to kill a man in battle was a disgrace in the ancient world (Judg. 9:54). The tables have turned, and now Jabin is subdued by the Israelites.

Where had the Kenites originally settled during the conquest? (Judg. 1:16)

What was the relationship between Jabin and Jael's husband Heber the Kenite? (Judg. 4:17)

How did Jael kill the sleeping Sisera? (Judg. 4:21)

BEHIND THE SCENES

On the surface, Jael simply appears a virtuous heroine who rises to the occasion to assist the Israelites. Actually her behavior is quite unusual in light of traditional Middle Eastern hospitality. Sisera came to Jael's tent because of the covenant of peace between Jabin and her husband Heber. Sisera expected refuge, not betrayal, at the residence of a friend. He also knew that pursuers would not look for him at a woman's tent because that would be a breach of etiquette. Jael next gave Sisera false hope by telling him not to fear. When she invited Sisera into her tent, Jael was offering him sanctuary and protection. Her offer of milk was a further sign of hospitality. Jael's murder of Sisera in her own tent would be viewed as the betrayal of friendship and trust that characterizes nomadic culture to this day. Jael thus defied accepted social conventions to demonstrate that her loyalty went beyond that to her husband and society, but to the God of Israel.[4]

What customs in modern society might be hindering your commitment to the Lord?

What actions can you take to demonstrate that your primary loyalty is to God and not to your job, church, or even your family?

DEBORAH AND BARAK'S SONG OF VICTORY (JUDG. 5:1–31)

Following the defeat of Sisera, Deborah and Barak sing a prophetic song of praise to God. Their song of victory resembles the one sung by Moses and Miriam following the successful crossing of the Red Sea (Ex. 15:1–21). These two songs may represent the oldest literary examples in the Bible. The song opens with praise to God for His intervention (Judg. 5:1–5). It next recounts the oppressive conditions under the Canaanites and how Deborah, a mother in Israel, arose to restore freedom in the land (5:6–11). The roles of the individual tribes in the victory are recalled. Although Zebulun and Naphtali were the primary participants in the conflict, several other tribes also helped. The tribes east of the Jordan as well as Dan and Asher are condemned for failing to help their brothers (5:12–18). The ferocity of the battle is now vividly described. Even the heavens are involved in the triumph (5:19–23). Jael is blessed for killing Sisera, and his death is described in vivid detail (5:24–27). In a dramatic twist Sisera's mother is depicted, waiting futilely for the return of her son (5:28–30). The song closes with a brief curse and blessing: the Lord's enemies are to perish while His friends are to shine brightly as the sun (5:31). Sisera's spectacular defeat brings forty years of peace for Israel.

What were the conditions in Israel before Deborah became judge? (Judg. 5:6–7)

Which tribes are named for helping to defeat Sisera? (Judg. 5:14–15, 18)

Near what river in the Jezreel Valley did the battle take place? (Judg. 5:21)

What was Sisera's mother expecting her son to bring home as spoils? (Judg. 5:30)

BEHIND THE SCENES

The New King James Version sets the song of Deborah and Barak in poetic form. Surprisingly, forty percent of the Old Testament is written as poetry. Whereas rhyming characterizes much of today's poetry, Hebrew poetry exhibits a characteristic called parallelism. The language and imagery of the first line is echoed in the succeeding line. When parallel lines convey approximately the same meaning, they represent synonymous paralleism. An example is Judges 5:4:

"LORD, when You *went out* from *Seir,*
When You *marched from* the field of *Edom.*"

Note the similar language that is italicized. The verbs mean the same thing; Seir and Edom refer to the same territory southeast of the Dead Sea.

Another type of parallelism is called antithetic, where the two lines express opposite thoughts. An example of this is Judges 5:31:

"Thus let all Your enemies perish, O LORD!
But let those who love Him be like the sun"

Note again the language that is underlined. This time the subjects are contrasted as well as their fate. Similar examples of parallelism are found in the song of Moses and Miriam (Ex. 15) as well as throughout the Psalms.[5]

FAITH ALIVE

What role does singing praise to God play in your public worship experience? In your private devotional time?

Why is expressing praise to God the natural response after receiving spiritual victory or promised blessing from Him?

At A Glance[6]

FOR YOUR INFO 21.14 — THE WOMEN OF JUDGES: ACCLAIMED AND ABUSED

The book of Judges illustrates a wide range of women's experiences in history, as the following table shows:

Women	Experience
Achsah	Caleb gave away his daughter Achsah as a reward for success in war (1.12,13). He also gave her land, which was unusual in that Hebrew women generally did not own land (1.14-16).
Deborah	She judged the nation for 40 years, enlisting Barak to lead the people to victory over the Canaanite general Sisera (4.1—5.31).
Jael	The wife of Heber the Kenite became a war hero by assassinating the general Sisera (4.17-22).
An Unnamed Concubine	Gideon's concubine gave birth to Abimelech (8.31), a man who brought great trouble to the nation.
An Unnamed Prostitute	She gave birth to a son, Jephthah, who was rejected by his half brothers, but later was recruited to deliver the nation from the Ammonites (11.1-33).
An Unnamed Daughter	Jephthah's daughter was presumably sacrificed as a burnt offering because of her father's rash vow (11.29-40).
An Unnamed, Barren Wife	Manoah's wife was chosen by God to be the mother of Samson, Israel's rescuer from the Philistines (13.2-25).
An Unnamed Philistine Wife	Samson's marriage to his wife from Timnah lasted one week before she was given to one of the young men who had been at Samson's party (14.1-20).
An Unnamed Prostitute	She used her wiles in an attempt to trap Samson in an ambush by the Philistines, but his physical strength confounded her efforts (16.1-3).
Delilah	Having captured Samson's affections, she wore down his resistance until he finally revealed the secret of his strength, to his own undoing (16.4-31).
An Unnamed Mother	Her son, Micah, stole 1,100 shekels of silver from her, but returned it. Together they fashioned idols that became a spiritual snare to a foolish Levite (17.1-13).
An Unnamed Concubine	She proved unfaithful to her Levite husband and returned to her father's house at Bethlehem. After the Levite retrieved her, she was gang-raped until she died, and her husband dismembered her, swearing revenge. The incident led to civil war in Israel (19.1-30).
Four Hundred Virgins of Mizpah	Captured as prizes in a civil war, they were given as wives to the wayward Benjamites (21.1-25).

1. Ruth A. Tucker and Walter Liefeld, *Daughters of the Church* (Grand Rapids: Zondervan Publishing House, 1987), 264–67.

2. *New International Dictionary of Biblical Archaeology* (Grand Rapids: Zondervan, 1983), 229–30, 437, "Hazor," "Tell."

3. *Nelson's New Illustrated Bible Dictionary* (Nashville: Thomas Nelson Publishers, 1995), 841–42, 844, "Minerals of the Bible, Iron, Tin."

4. Herbert Wolf, "Judges," in *Expositor's Bible Commentary*, Vol. 3 (Grand Rapids: Zondervan Publishing House, 1992), 407.

5. *Nelson's New Illustrated Bible Dictionary*, 1012–13, "Poetry."

6. *Word in Life Study Bible* (Nashville: Thomas Nelson Publishers, 1996), 471, "The Women of Judges."

Lesson 9/Overcoming Fear in Realizing God's Promise
Judges 6:1—8:35

Fear gripped this Oklahoma schoolboy as the teacher approached his desk. "Name the first five presidents of the United States," she asked. He knew the answer, but his tongue froze and the words stuck in his mouth.

What a burden—to carry a name that meant "spoken word," yet be unable to speak because of a speech problem. Throughout his youth, he only got a bad grade when he was called upon to recite orally. "Something inside was making me afraid, tormenting me with fear that I would never be able to talk like other children," he recalls.

His mother, however, believed that one day her son would preach the gospel. She prophesied that his speech impediment would be healed and that multitudes would be touched by her son's ministry. The fulfillment of that prophecy occurred when her teenage son lay dying of tuberculosis. At a meeting one evening a healing evangelist commanded the foul tormenting disease to come out of the young man. Instantly his lungs opened and the pain was gone. Shouts of "I'm healed! I'm healed!" rang through the tent. The evangelist asked the teenager to describe what God had done for him. "To my utter amazement and joy, the words no longer stuck on my throat. All fear that I could not talk without stammering was gone, and the words flowed from my lips like a spring gushing up from the earth."

Oral Roberts indeed fulfilled his mother's vision. After conquering his fear of speaking, Roberts has preached to millions of people around the world.[1]

In this lesson we will meet an Israelite who also had to conquer fear before God could use him to deliver His people. At his calling Gideon was hiding underground in a wine press threshing wheat. After overcoming his fear, Gideon became one of Israel's most effective judges.

GIDEON'S CALL (JUDG. 6:1–40)

The next foreign power to oppress Israel is the Midianites. They enforce a scorched-earth policy that keeps the Israelites in poverty for seven years. When Israel cries out to God, He first sends an unnamed prophet to the Israelites exhorting them not to fear the Amorite gods but to obey Him. Next the Angel of the Lord appears to a man in Manasseh named Gideon. Out of fear of the Midianites, he is threshing his wheat secretly in an underground winepress. Gideon cannot believe the Angel's announcement that he is to be Israel's deliverer. After sacrificing to the Angel, Gideon builds an altar called The-Lord-Is-Peace—*Yahweh Shalom*. Before His departure, the Angel instructs Gideon to tear down his family's altar of Baal. Under the cover of night Gideon takes ten servants and destroys the altar. The city leaders of Ophrah seek to kill Gideon for his deed, but his father successfully intercedes in his son's behalf. When the Spirit of the Lord falls upon Gideon, he mobilizes the northern tribes against the Midianites. For final confirmation of his mission to save Israel Gideon twice puts out a fleece before God.

What reminder of deliverance did God give the Israelites through His prophet? (Judg. 6:8–9)

What ironic title did the Angel give to Gideon? (Judg. 6:12)

What nickname was Gideon given following his destruction of the altar of Baal? (Judg. 6:32)

In what ways was God to change the fleece of wool so that Gideon knew his prayer was answered? (Judg. 6:37–40)

 FAITH ALIVE

Do you ever feel like a "nobody" in your church, and that God could never use you for anything?

How does Gideon's example provide encouragement that you are a "somebody" to God and that He wants to use you to advance His kingdom?

 PROBING THE DEPTHS

Gideon asks a question that every Christian asks at one time, "If the LORD is with us, why then has all this happened to us?" (Judg. 6:13). Today we might express it as, "Why do bad things happen to God's people?" Some suggest that a lack of faith or God's discipline is why a crippling accident or a life-threatening disease has occurred. In Gideon's case disobedience and idolatry *were* the reasons for Israel's punishment. But in other situations such a response is too simplistic, since we all know Spirit-filled believers who have suffered personal loss and hardship.

Recently our local newspaper carried a story about a Christian truck driver—close to retirement and with an exemplary driving record—who was killed when a minivan wandered across the freeway median. Hanging from his rearview mirror was a chain that read "Jesus Saves." In such situations we can become like Job's comforters with all the answers, or we can simply acknowledge our lack of understanding why these tragedies occur. Suffering remains a part of this fallen world. Even Jesus warned His disciples that they would endure tribu-lation, but they were to be of good cheer, for He had overcome the world (John 16:33). God does not require that we defend His goodness and omnipotence in light of the existence of evil and pain—the theology of **theodicy.** Rather it is our attitude and response that are most important to Him. For God wants us to praise and worship Him not only in our triumphs but also in our seeming defeats. Ultimately we throw ourselves on the mercy and grace of a loving God who works all things together for the good of us who love Him (Rom. 8:38).

Can you recall a time of personal pain and suffering when you wondered where God was?

What spiritual resources helped you to get through this difficult period?

How do you reconcile the problem of a good God allowing bad things to happen to Christians?

 ## FAITH ALIVE

When God called Gideon, he was living in a state of fear. He was fearful because of his job, his family, and his nation. Only at God's word, "Peace be with you; do not fear" (Judg. 6:23), did Gideon's fear leave.

What things or situations in your life cause you to be fearful?

What God-given opportunities have you passed over because you feared failure would result?

How is Gideon's example helping you to overcome fear?

Read 2 Timothy 1:7. What does this Scripture verse tell us about fear and how to overcome it?

 PROBING THE DEPTHS

If we are honest enough to admit it, we have all put out a fleece before God at one time or another. Why? Because we have wanted to know God's will about something. So in the time of waiting, because His answer was unclear, we put out a fleece, following the example of Gideon. Recently I was praying about a teaching opportunity at a certain Christian university. Since I tend to become impatient during times of transition, I wanted to hurry the decision-making process along. The university's president was coming to my city to speak at a church dedication. He had received a copy of one of my recommendation letters, so I put a fleece out before the Lord. If this president called me while in town, I would know it was God's will for me to teach at this university. Unfortunately, no call came in the midst of the president's busy schedule. Although I was disappointed, I knew this was not the end of the matter, for God had yet to answer definitively. Over a month later the job offer came through normal channels, and I accepted it. My fleece failed to prove anything, since God knew that my impatience was driving my need to have an answer **now.**

What has been your experience with putting out a fleece before God?

Do you think putting out a fleece is still a valid way for Christians to receive guidance?

GIDEON'S ARMY (JUDG. 7:1–25)

Thirty-two thousand men respond to Gideon's call to mobilize. What a mighty army to fight the Midianites! However, God's unorthodox battle plan comes into play again: He instructs Gideon to send home 22,000 who are fearful. At least 10,000 still remain but that number is reduced to 300 when Gideon examines how they drink water. Only a few scoop the water with their hands, lapping it like dogs; most kneel carelessly by the water leaving their backs exposed to the enemy. This 99 percent reduction in troop strength again demonstrates who the Commander of the army is. That night Gideon sneaks into the Midianite camp and overhears one soldier describe his dream of Israelite victory. After Gideon returns to his men, he splits them into three companies and posts them around the enemy camp, their only "weapons" being a shophar, a pitcher, and a torch. At Gideon's signal the men blow their shophars and break the pitchers that cover the lit torches. This surprise sound-and-light show throws the army of Midian into a panic, with its troops accidentally killing one another. Gideon recalls the Israelite warriors from their homes to chase the retreating Midianites. Victory is secure when two Midianite princes are captured and killed.

Why did God send so many Israelite warriors back to their homes? (Judg. 7:2)

What do you think the test about drinking water proved about the fighting abilities of the 300 remaining men? (Judg. 7:5–7)

How did the dream and interpretation of the two Midianite men convince Gideon that victory was at hand? (Judg. 7:13–14)

What did the Israelites cry out when they blew their shophars and broke their pitchers? (Judg. 7:20)

FAITH ALIVE

At times God reduces our physical and material resources so that we are forced to depend totally on Him.

Can you recall a time when you were thrust completely on God to solve a problem? What happened to the resources on which you normally depended?

What were your feelings toward God at the time, and what carried you through?

What was the outcome of the situation, and how did God receive glory for the victory?

GIDEON'S VICTORY (JUDG. 8:1–21)

Victory over the Midianites quickly degenerated into accusations against Gideon. The Ephraimites thought they did not receive their proper share of the battle's glory and spoils. Gideon shows remarkable leadership skills in the way he deflects their criticism. He resumes pursuit of Midian's two kings Zebah and Zalmunna east of the Jordan. After failing to gain provisions for his famished men at Succoth and Penuel, Gideon vows reprisals on the cities once his fight with the Midianites is over. He finally overtakes the Midianite army and routs them, taking the kings captive. On his return to Ophrah he punishes the elders of Succoth with thorns and kills all the men of Penuel.

Because Zebah and Zalmunna had killed his stepbrothers at Tabor, Gideon kills the two Midianite kings with his sword.

How does Gideon deflect the criticism of the Ephraimites? (Judg. 8:3)

Why do you think the men of Succoth and Penuel refused to give food to the Israelites? (Judg. 8:6, 8)

How did Gideon learn the names of Succoth's elders in order to punish them? (Judg. 8:14)

Who was Gideon's son, and what did he fail to do? (Judg. 8:20)

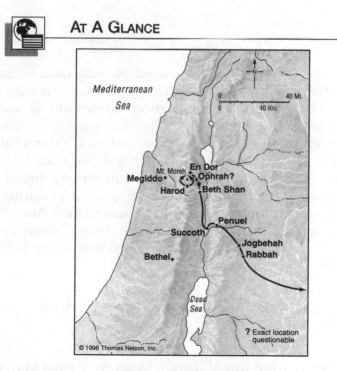

AT A GLANCE

GIDEON'S CAMPAIGN[2]

FAITH ALIVE

Being a leader in God's army is not easy. Both success and failure can invite criticism. If you are a leader in your church, have you ever been criticized, and how did you respond to that criticism?

Have you ever disagreed with your pastor or other church leader over an issue, and how did you handle that disagreement?

What does Gideon's response teach us about handling conflict among God's people?

GIDEON'S APOSTASY (JUDG. 8:22–35)

When the Israelites invite Gideon to rule over them, he answers in the negative, asserting that it is the Lord who shall rule over the nation. Gideon's good confession is quickly negated by his actions. He gathers golden earrings and other valuables captured from the Midianites and molds them into an ephod that is set up in Ophrah. The ephod becomes an idolatrous image in Israel, as the people begin to worship it as a shrine. Gideon judges the nation for forty years, and during that time he has seventy sons. He also has a son named Abimelech, who is born to his concubine in Shechem. After Gideon's death Israel returns to worshiping the Baals and fails to show kindness to his family.

With whom did the Israelites want Gideon to rule? (Judg. 8:22)

What booty from the Midianite kings were used in making the ephod? (Judg. 8:26)

Who was the son of Gideon born to a concubine in Shechem? (Judg. 8:31)

FAITH ALIVE

Have you ever heard the expression, "He sure talks a good walk"? Often what we say doesn't line up with our life. This was Gideon's problem: his confession of God's lordship did not convert over into appropriate actions.

Are there any areas in your Christian life where your talk is better than your walk?

What steps can you take to bring your confession in line with your action?

BEHIND THE SCENES

Marriage customs in the ancient world permitted both polygamy and concubines. Although God's plan at creation was monogamy (Gen. 2:23–24), the Israelites unfortunately adopted the marital practices of their heathen neighbors. The ancient Hebrews placed great value on large families. So when a wife was childless, her husband would frequently father children through a female slave called a concubine. Abraham's brother Nahor took a concubine named Reumah (Gen. 22:24). Abraham took Hagar as a concubine, and Ishmael resulted from their union (Gen. 16:3–16). Much strife has resulted from this ill-conceived relationship. Other figures who had concubines include Jacob (Gen. 35:22), Eliphaz (Gen. 36:12), and Saul (2 Sam. 3:7). Solomon was renowned for his many foreign concubines. The idolatrous religions they introduced into the king's household led to his downfall (1 Kin. 11:1–13). While not condoning such behavior, God recognized the times for what they were and provided for humane regulation of such marital practices in the law (Ex. 21:7–11; Deut. 21:10–14). The New Testament adamantly affirms that marriage is to be one time with one woman. All other sexual activity, even for procreation, is fornication and adultery (Matt. 5:31–32; 1 Cor. 7:10–16).[3]

1. Oral Roberts. *Expect a Miracle: My Life and Ministry, An Autobiography* (Nashville: Thomas Nelson Publishers, 1995), 19, 34.
2. *Spirit-Filled Life® Bible* (Nashville: Thomas Nelson Publishers, 1991), 355, "Gideon's Campaign."
3. *Nelson's New Illustrated Bible Dictionary* (Nashville: Thomas Nelson Publishers, 1995), 294, "Concubine."

Lesson 10/Overcoming Rejection in Realizing God's Promise
Judges 9:1—12:15

Rejection can be a real obstacle to healing and renewal. In his book *Love, Acceptance & Forgiveness,* Jerry Cook tells about a prominent pastor in his community who got involved in an adulterous relationship. His wife divorced him, and his church fell apart when the affair became public. A year and a half after the incident Cook received a call early one Sunday morning from this former pastor. He asked if he and his new wife could attend Cook's church that morning. For eight months the couple had been trying to attend a service in the community, but pastor after pastor had rejected them, refusing to extend fellowship to them.

Cook invited the couple to the service, and although things were initially awkward, God began a great cleansing and healing in their lives. In the weeks that followed, Cook and his elders began to show love to this fallen brother. He responded with godly sorrow and repentance, asking these church leaders for forgiveness. Instead of rejecting this man, Cook accepted him despite his sin. He saw God restore the man to wholeness, with the result that he is now back in ministry.[1]

In this lesson we will meet two men who both experienced rejection because of the sexual excesses of their fathers. The first, Abimelech, ended up being destroyed by his ambition and pride, while the second, Jephthah, became a great judge who brought deliverance to Israel.

THE RISE AND FALL OF ABIMELECH (JUDG. 9:1–57)

As the son of Gideon's concubine, Abimelech has no legal claim to his father's inheritance and is rejected by his half-brothers. However, he has aspirations to rule and talks his mother's family into supporting his bid. He hires a team of assassins for seventy shekels to help him kill Gideon's seventy rightful heirs at Ophrah. Only the youngest son Jotham escapes the massacre. As Abimelech is being installed as king at Shechem, Jotham climbs to the top of Mount Gerizim and, to those gathered below, tells a fable about the trees choosing a leader. Before he flees, Jotham pronounces a curse upon Abimelech along with the men of Shechem and Beth Millo. The alliance between Abimelech and the Shechemites soon breaks down. Laying ambush to the city, Abimelech's forces kill many of the defenders and burn those who seek refuge in the stronghold of the temple of Berith. Later Abimelech attacks Thebez and again seeks to burn its residents gathered in the city's stronghold. When he approaches the tower door, a woman drops a millstone, crushing Abimelech's head. The man who would be king dies at the hand of his armorbearer. Jotham's curse on Abimelech and the men of Shechem is indeed fulfilled.

In what manner were the half-brothers of Abimelech killed? (Judg. 9:5)

What are the four trees mentioned in the fable and to which of them is Abimelech compared? (Judg. 9:8–14)

Why did Abimelech ask his armorbearer to thrust him through with his sword? (Judg. 9:54)

FAITH ALIVE

A feeling of rejection can provoke various responses in people. In Jephthah's case, to be discussed later in this lesson, he overcame rejection to lead his people to victory. However, Abimelech's rejection by his father's family turned into unbridled jealousy and ambition. Instead of waiting for God to install him as leader, Abimelech forced the issue through manipulation and bloodshed. Therefore his kingship over Shechem was always unstable, and his subjects eventually turned against him.

Do you know someone who handled rejection improperly? What was the result?

Have you ever been rejected by a family member or a coworker? If so, what was your response?

Have you ever forced open a door of opportunity because of ambition instead of waiting for God to open it? What did you learn from that experience?

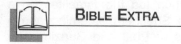

BIBLE EXTRA

The fable is one of several storytelling devices used in the Bible. Other such devices are allegory and parable. Fables are stories in which animals and plants speak and act like people. One of the most famous collections of such stories is *Aesop's Fables*.[2] Besides Jotham's story, there are two other fables in the Old Testament. The first is found in 2 Kings 14:9. First, read the surrounding context in verses 1–22. What are the plant, tree, and animal mentioned, and what do they represent?

Why does King Jehoash tell this fable to King Amaziah? (2 Kin. 14:10)

The second fable is found in Ezekiel 17:1–24. Again, what are the bird, tree, and plant mentioned? (Ezek. 17:3–8)

What do these things represent? (Ezek. 17:12–18)

Why did God give this fable to Israel? (Ezek. 17:19–21)

BEHIND THE SCENES

The city of Shechem was important to Israel's history. Here the Lord appeared to Abraham and promised that He would give his descendants the Promised Land (Gen. 12:7). Later Jacob built an altar in Shechem to mark his safe return to Canaan and bought a parcel of land upon which to pitch his tent (Gen. 33:18–19). He dug a well upon it, which Jesus visited over a millennium later (John 4:12).

After the victory at Ai, Joshua led the Israelites on a twenty-mile journey northward to Shechem. Looming above Shechem are the twin mountains of Ebal and Gerizim. The mountains rise approximately three thousand feet from the valley floor, which is about two miles wide. Here Joshua conducted the covenant renewal ceremony, in which half of the Israelites stood atop each mountain, some speaking words of blessing, some words of curse (Josh. 8:30–35). It was from a ledge, called "Jotham's pulpit," halfway up Mount Gerizim that tradition says Jotham proclaimed his fable to the Shechemites below.[3]

These two biblical accounts seem a physical impossibility without the benefit of modern amplification equipment. Yet Alan Redpath suggests that the audience could hear the speakers. "Any traveler to the land of Palestine today can tell you that you can stand on the top of Mount Ebal and talk with someone on the top of Mount Gerizim, almost without raising your voice, so perfect are the natural acoustics. The amphitheater provided by the valley is utterly natural and complete, and voices ring across it from peak to peak."[4]

MORE JUDGES AND FURTHER APOSTASY (JUDG. 10:1–18)

After Abimelech, two minor judges arise—Tola of the tribe of Issachar and Jair of Manasseh. Rather than being military leaders who save Israel from her enemies, both administer justice within Israelite society. Once again the people of Israel apostatize and serve the gods of the surrounding nations. In His anger God allows the Philistines and Ammonites to harass and oppress the Israelites. When they cry out to God in repentance, He reminds the people how time after time He has delivered them, only to be forsaken for other gods. Yet again they put away their foreign gods and begin to serve the true God. In His great mercy He responds to the people's misery by putting the hope of deliverance into their hearts. Israel gathers expectantly for battle and begins to look for someone to lead them against the Ammonites.

Where did Tola exercise his judgeship? (Judg. 10:1)

What was the unique thing about Jair related to the number thirty? (Judg. 10:4)

Where did the armies of Israel and Ammon gather for battle? (Judg. 10:17)

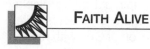 FAITH ALIVE

God reminds the Israelites of seven enemies from whom He has already delivered them (Judg. 10:11–12). Why is it important in the midst of an oppressive situation to recall God's previous works of deliverance?

Name several occasions when God has provided relief for you from some problem.

•

•

•

•

How does the recollection of such deliverances help you through any present difficulties you are encountering?

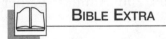 BIBLE EXTRA

Judges 10:7 states that the Lord's anger was hot against Israel. How can a holy God who is a spiritual being display human emotions? Such language is a figure of speech called an **anthropopathism,** which is the depiction of God with human feelings. Look up the following Scripture verses and identify other examples of anthropopathism in the Old Testament.[5]

Exodus 20:5

1 Samuel 15:11

Psalm 77:9   *Has God forgotten to be merciful? Has he in anger withheld his Compassion*

Psalm 103:8   *the Lord is Compassionate and gracious slow to anger abounding in love*

Psalm 147:5   *Great is our Lord and mighty in power his understanding his no limit.*

Jonah 4:2   *He prayed to the Lord, O Lord is this not what I said when I was still at home? that is why I was so quick to flee to tarshish. I knew that you are a gracious and Compassionate, God slow to anger and abounding in love a God who relents from sending Calamity*

What does the Bible's use of such language say to you about God?

Do anthropopathisms in the Bible suggest anything about how God responds to the actions of His children?

JEPHTHAH'S VOW AND VICTORY (JUDG. 11:1–40)

Jephthah, like Abimelech, is born outside the bond of marriage, with his mother being a harlot. Rejected from a share in the family inheritance, he is driven out of the house by his stepbrothers. Jephthah gathers a band of outlaws around him for the purpose of raiding. When the Ammonites threaten Israel, the elders of Gilead ask Jephthah to lead them in battle. In spite of his earlier rejection by the Gileadites, Jephthah agrees to lead the Israelites if they appoint him their head and commander. This they eagerly do.

Jephthah tries to avoid a battle, but the king of Ammon is determined to recapture what was taken earlier by Moses. Jephthah reminds the king that it was not Israel's intention to take the land east of the Jordan. But because the Amorites refused to allow the Israelites safe passage, Moses was forced to dispossess the occupants. The Ammonite king refuses to back down. The Spirit then empowers Jephthah, and he leads the Israelite army to a total rout of the Ammonites.

Before the battle Jephthah vowed to the Lord that if victory is granted, he will offer as a sacrifice the first thing that comes out of his house upon his return. Unfortunately, his daughter is the first to emerge, dancing and rejoicing as she greets him. Jephthah keeps his word to the Lord, although he now realizes his vow was ill-spoken. His daughter obediently submits to its fulfillment, and Jephthah loses the companionship of his only child as well as the possibility of any descendants.

Which kings refused to allow the Israelites to pass through their territory? (Judg. 11:17–21)

What is the name of the god of the Ammonites? (Judg. 11:24)

For how many years did Israel possess the land on the banks of the Arnon River? (Judg. 11:26)

How many cities did Jephthah capture from the Ammonites? (Judg. 11:33)

What did Jephthah's daughter request to do before fulfilling her father's vow? (Judg. 11:37–38)

BIBLE EXTRA

Vows were often made by the Israelites, particularly in times of trouble. They were voluntary pledges to God that bound a person to do some specific act or to behave in a certain manner, but only if God answered the petitioner's request. Vows were usually made in expectation of God's favor (Gen. 28:20) or in thanksgiving for His blessings (Ps. 116:12–14). They were to be carefully considered before being made (Prov. 20:25). Once made vows were carefully regulated (Num. 30). Vows would be paid before the congregation at the tabernacle (Deut. 12:6, 11) or later at the temple (Ps. 22:25).[6] In the following passages identify the persons who made vows and note the nature of their vows.

PETITIONER   VOW

Genesis 28:20–22

Numbers 21:2–3

1 Samuel 1:11

2 Samuel 15:7–8

Psalm 132:2–5

Acts 18:18

PROBING THE DEPTHS

One of the most bizarre incidents in the Bible is Jephthah's vow to sacrifice whatever came out first through the door of his house. Ancient dwellings accommodated both people and livestock. A typical two-story house provided living quarters on the upper level and storage and work rooms on the ground level. During times of war or bad weather the most valuable livestock would also be sheltered in the house. Clearly Jephthah had such an animal in mind, never imagining that his daughter would emerge.

There are two interpretations as to how Jephthah fulfilled his vow. The first suggests that Jephthah actually presented his daughter as a human burnt offering, even as Abraham attempted to do (Gen. 22:1–13). His daughter's acceptance of her fate is reminiscent of Isaac's willingness to be placed on the altar. Because of the moral decline in the land, this judge was simply imitating the abominable practice of child sacrifice performed by the very people he destroyed—the Ammonites (see 2 Kin. 3:27). Even though Jephthah's pledge was perhaps presumptuous and brought much grief to both father and daughter, he could not go back on his word to the Lord. Thus Jephthah carried out his vow to offer up a burnt offering.

The second interpretation suggests that Jephthah's daughter remained a perpetual virgin and dedicated her life to serving God at Israel's central sanctuary (see 1 Sam. 2:22). This perspective is very appealing for several reasons. First, although the Israelites had compromised with their neighbors, there is no indication that they had sunk to the depths of human sacrifice. Their God had prohibited the Israelites from sacrificing humans (Lev. 18:21; Deut. 12:31). Jephthah's detailed knowledge of Israel's history (Judg. 11:13–27) strongly suggests that he was aware of the law's prohibition against human sacrifice. Second, the author of Judges indicates no outrage at this point, as is expressed later at the mutilation of the concubine's body (Judg. 19:30). Surely child sacrifice would have likewise evoked such a horror. Third, the vow follows the Spirit of the Lord coming upon Jephthah. It is inconceivable that a person empowered by the Spirit would commit such an abominable act. Fourth, the passage mentions three times that his daughter was a virgin and would remain one (Judg. 11:37, 38, 39). For a woman to be childless was a major reproach in the ancient world. In Judges the only information usually given about the minor judges is the number of their sons and daughters. Although Jephthah had secured a great victory, he would have no heirs to perpetuate his name and his clan would become extinct. Fifth, a custom developed in Israel to commemorate Jephthah's daughter. For four days each year the women recalled her lamentable fate. Given the emphasis on memorials throughout Joshua and Judges, it is inconceivable that a barbaric act of human sacrifice would be celebrated for generations. Both perspectives have their strengths and weaknesses, and we will never know what really happened. For Jephthah and his daughter either outcome was a great family tragedy.[7]

Which of these two interpretations seems most plausible from your reading of the passage?

Can you discover any other arguments that suggest one perspective is more likely than the other?

 FAITH ALIVE

Jephthah's vow and its problematic outcome suggest a number of applications for us today. Zeal without knowledge may be dangerous; hasty commitments without forethought may bring grief; foolish statements without wisdom may produce tragedy.

Can you recall a time when your zeal for God led to problems?

What were these problems, and how did you resolve them?

Do you have a tendency to make hasty commitments? If so, how do you get out of them?

CONFLICT WITH EPHRAIM (JUDG. 12:1–14)

Jephthah's victory should have brought great rejoicing in Israel. Instead it reopens old tribal wounds between the people of Gilead and the tribe of Ephraim. The Ephraimites charge Jephthah with failing to mobilize them for the war against the Ammonites. In response Jephthah accuses the tribe of Ephraim of failing to support him. Their conflict erupts into a civil war with the men of Gilead prevailing. As the Ephraimites attempt to retreat across the Jordan River at a ford held by the Gileadites, there is a great slaughter. Because of speech differences in their dialect, the Ephraimites fail to say the "sh" in "Shibboleth" ("flowing stream") and therefore are identified as the enemy. Jephthah's reign is brief, only six years. Born of a harlot, Jephthah leaves no heir, his daughter dying a virgin. Three minor judges follow: Ibzan from the tribe of Judah, Elon of the tribe of Zebulun, and Abdon of the tribe of Ephraim.

What did the men of Ephraim threaten to do to Jephthah? (Judg. 12:1)

What was unique about the family of Ibzan? (Judg. 12:9)

What was unique about the family of Abdon? (Judg. 12:14)

FAITH ALIVE

Division among God's people brings reproach to God and his kingdom. Unfortunately, church splits are a reality and are often instigated over petty issues motivated by pride and stubbornness. Often no side emerges as a winner in the struggle. The church and its pastor are weakened, and their reputation in the community forever tarnished. Have you ever been involved in a church split, and what was its cause?

What was the outcome of the church split?

What did you learn from the experience about how to deal with conflict?

BEHIND THE SCENES

What was the significance of Abdon's children and grandchildren riding on seventy donkeys? We likewise read in Judges that Jair's sons (10:4) and an unnamed Levite (19:3) also rode donkeys. In the ancient world donkeys were not the objects of ridicule we think of today, but the preferred mode of transportation for the rich and famous (Judg. 5:10). They were likewise a mark of royalty. During times of peace it was customary that the king rode a donkey (Zech. 9:9). Horses were ridden only during times of war. For the sons of the judges to be riding about on donkeys suggests a time of peace and prosperity in Israel. When Jesus made His triumphal entry into Jerusalem, He rode on a young donkey (Matt. 21:1–9). The prophetic and cultural significance of the donkey was surely not lost on the crowd that acclaimed Him as the Son of David.[8]

1. Jerry Cook with Stanley C. Baldwin, *Love, Acceptance & Forgiveness* (Ventura, CA: Regal Books, 1979), 9–11.

2. *Nelson's New Illustrated Bible Dictionary* (Nashville: Thomas Nelson Publishers, 1995), 438, "Fable."

3. Ibid., 374, "Ebal," 489, "Gerizim."

4. Alan Redpath, *Victorious Christian Living* (Westwood, NJ: Fleming H. Revell Company, 1955), 126.

5. *Nelson's New Illustrated Bible Dictionary,* 79, "Anthropopathism."

6. Ibid., 1297, "Vow."

7. *Spirit-Filled Life® Bible* (Nashville: Thomas Nelson Publishers, 1991), 367, notes on Judges 11:31 and 11:39.

8. *Word in Life Study Bible* (Nashville: Thomas Nelson Publishers, 1996), 458, "Donkeys: A Mark of Royalty."

Lesson 11/Overcoming Lust in Realizing God's Promise
Judges 13:1—16:31

It seems like a no-brainer. Pastoring a growing church and attending X-rated movies are activities that don't go together. Mike Fehlauer, however, was leading a double life. Although he had a beautiful wife and two lovely children, Mike was enslaved to sexual compulsion.

It had started innocently enough. One day Mike was picking up trash in his yard. One item was a paperback book, and when he looked at its content, he realized it was pornographic. Yet he could not put the book down, and its explicit sexual imagery became imprinted in his memory. Those images became the fixation of his dreams and fantasies. Although Mike read his Bible and prayed for deliverance, he realized he was losing the spiritual battle. His city in Florida was full of strip joints, adult bookstores, and X-rated movie theaters, and soon Mike became a regular customer at these. One day he visited a massage parlor just to check it out, and its lure brought him back for what was to be his first act of adultery.

Throughout this time he continued his pastoral duties—preaching, counseling, and visitation. Mike had compartmentalized his life between the sacred and the profane. As the downward spiral continued, Mike became desperate. One Sunday evening he sat in his car staring at his church; pointed at his head was a gun for committing suicide. God somehow intervened, and Mike put the gun down and drove home. Several days later he finally confessed everything to his wife. With her support, Mike began the slow healing process to break the bondage of his sexual addiction. Today Mike is back in the ministry, helping others receive deliverance from sexual and other types of addictions.[1]

Our character in this lesson—a familiar hero from Sunday school—likewise had a problem with lust. Although God used Samson as a judge, his effectiveness was limited because his sexual compulsions led to his premature death.

Samson's Promised Birth (Judg. 13:1–24)

Israel's cycle of apostasy next brings the nation under the bondage of the Philistines for forty years. Living amidst the tribe of Dan was a godly man, Manoah, and his wife, who is childless. The Angel of the Lord appears to the woman and announces that she will bear a son who will deliver Israel from the Philistines. This angelic birth announcement resembles that made to Abraham and Sarah (Gen. 18:10–15), Zacharias (Luke 1:11–20), and Mary (Luke 1:26–38). During the pregnancy she is to take a special vow so that her son will be set apart as a Nazirite from conception. When Manoah hears of his wife's marvelous encounter, he too desires to hear this announcement from the angel. The angel graciously appears to the couple and repeats his wonderful news. Manoah prepares a goat for sacrifice; and when it is offered, the angel ascends toward heaven in the flame from the altar. At his birth the baby is called Samson (meaning "Distinguished"). God blesses this young boy and soon the Spirit of the Lord begins to move upon him at Mahaneh Dan.

What three prohibitions did the angel give Manoah's wife? (Judg. 13:4–5)

1.

2.

3.

What name did the angel relate to Manoah? (Judg. 13:18; cf. Is. 9:6)

What was the response of Manoah and his wife to the angel's ascension in the flame? (Judg. 13:20)

Why did Manoah think that he and his wife would die? (Judg. 13:22)

BEHIND THE SCENES

From his conception Samson was called to be a Nazirite. The Nazirites were a group of men and women who took vows to set themselves apart as an offering unto the Lord. Numbers 6:1–21 lists the regulations that governed this special group open to all Israelites.

Three regulations characterized the Nazirite vow: (1) abstention from all fruit of the grapevine, either fresh grapes or raisins or wine; (2) forsaking all haircuts; and (3) avoidance of all dead bodies. The vow was for a fixed time, usually 30 to 90 days. When this period was over, the Nazirite appeared before the priest to make the prescribed offerings. The Nazirite then cut his or her hair and burned it, thereby bringing full release from the vow. Samson, Samuel, and John the Baptist were the only lifelong Nazirites in the Bible, with each dedicated to the Lord by their parents before their birth.

Unfortunately, Samson broke the three cardinal regulations of the Nazirites. At his wedding feast Samson probably drank wine, a staple of such occasions (Judg. 14:10; see John 2:1–10). When Samson stopped to look at the lion that he killed, he touched the carcass as he retrieved the honey (Judg. 14:9). He also used as a weapon the jawbone of a freshly killed donkey (Judg. 15:15–16). And after he revealed the secret of his strength to Delilah, the Philistines cut off his hair (Judg. 16:19).

With such callous disregard for his vows, Samson spurned not only his godly parents, but also the God who had supernaturally endowed him to be a judge for the deliverance of Israel.[2]

FAITH ALIVE

Is there still a place in the Christian life for a Nazirite-type vow? Paul seems to suggest so in his first letter to the Corinthians. Addressing married believers, he speaks of a time when couples should forgo sexual relations in order to fast and pray. They should agree to a specific period so that Satan cannot use their abstinence as a means of temptation. Then such couples should resume normal marital relations (1 Cor. 7:5). Such an act of consecration may also be practiced by unmarried believers.

Have you ever set aside a special time of prayer and fasting to seek God?

What normal activities did you abstain from during this period?

What were the spiritual consequences of this special time?

When are you planning again to set yourself apart for such a spiritual season?

PROBING THE DEPTHS

Does human life begin at conception or birth? This debate centered around the issue of abortion continues to rage in society today. The story of Samson's birth again demonstrates that from God's perspective life begins at conception. The angel tells Manoah's wife that she is to become a Nazirite even before she has sexual relations with her husband and conceives. This is to ensure that her promised son is sanctified from grape products or unclean food at his beginning in the womb (Judg. 13:4). Whatever inconvenience or hardship such a vow placed on Samson's mother during her pregnancy was set aside to obey God so she might see her son's blessed birth.

What other perspectives on conception and birth does this story suggest to you?

Have you had to deal personally with the issue of abortion in relation to friends or family members? How did the teaching of the Bible help in making the important ethical decisions involved?

BEHIND THE SCENES

Who were the mighty Philistines, feared by the Israelites for hundreds of years? Although little is known about their origins, Genesis 10:14 suggests that they came from Caphtor, usually identified as the island of Crete. Early Egyptian records mention the Philistines as a sea people defeated by Pharaoh Rameses III in a naval battle in 1188 B.C. Abraham encountered the Philistines in Canaan and lived with them for a time at Gerar (Gen. 20:1–2; 26:1).

Although Abraham's relationship with the Philistines was peaceful, during Joshua's conquest this people became Israel's fiercest enemy. Their political base was five cities along the Mediterranean coast—Ashkelon, Ashdod, Ekron, Gath, and Gaza. Because the Philistines possessed superior iron weapons, the tribe of Dan, which received the coastal plain as its possession, could not dislodge them (Josh. 13:2–3). During the period of the judges the Philistines oppressed the tribes of Dan and Judah, their neighbors to the east (Judg. 13:1–2; 15:9). Samson's deliverance was a welcome respite from this oppression, but because of his failure to control his fleshly desires, this superhero failed to secure any long-term peace for Israel. Later, in the time of the judge Eli, the Philistines captured the ark of the covenant, but returned it after divine judgment in the form of hemorrhoids came upon its captors (1 Sam. 4:1—6:19).

The ongoing Philistine threat prompted the Israelites to demand a king (1 Sam. 8:19–20). The history of Saul's monarchy is filled with constant conflict with the Philistines (1 Sam. 13:1—14:46). In one such battle David killed the Philistine giant Goliath in the Elah Valley (1 Sam. 17). In the struggle between Saul and David, David allied himself with the Philistines for a time (1 Sam. 27—29). Both Saul and Jonathan were killed in a battle with the Philistines at Mount Gilboa (1 Sam. 31). It was finally under King David that the Philistines were subdued and their oppression of the Israelites stopped (2 Sam. 21:15–22; 1 Chr. 18:1; 20:4–8). The Philistines were thus the most persistent thorn in Israel's side for generations.[3]

AT A GLANCE[4]

THE PHILISTINES

SAMSON'S STRENGTH AND WEAKNESSES (JUDG. 14:1–20)

Samson is attracted to a Philistine woman in Timnah and asks his parents to arrange a marriage with her. Despite their objections about marrying a non-Israelite, Samson persists with his request. Although God does not endorse Samson's unholy libido, nevertheless He uses his weakness to bring deliverance to Israel. On a visit to his fiancee, Samson kills a lion with his bare hands and leaves it along the road. On another visit Samson stops to look at the dead lion and discovers a honeycomb in its carcass.

When his wedding feast finally comes, Samson poses a riddle concerning the lion and its honey to the thirty young male guests. The winner of the wager will receive thirty changes of clothing. As the seven-day feast progresses the men become more and more desperate to solve the riddle. Finally, they threaten Samson's fiancee with the burning of her family home if she fails to secure the answer. Her persistent nagging pays off, and Samson at last reveals to her the solution to the riddle. When the young men supply Samson with the correct answer, he knows immediately how they obtained it. The Spirit of the Lord comes upon Samson, and he angrily kills thirty men in Ashkelon to secure the clothing necessary to pay up on the wager. Abandoning his bride for disclosing the riddle's answer, Samson returns to his parents' home.

Why did Samson's parents object to his choice of a wife? (Judg. 14:3)

How did Samson acquire the supernatural strength to kill the lion? (Judg. 14:6)

What happened to Samson's wife after he returned home? (Judg. 14:20)

WORD WEALTH

Samson courted the Philistine woman in Timnah because she **pleased** him (Judg. 14:3, 7). The Hebrew expression *yasherah be'enay* (Strong's #3477, 5869) is an idiom literally meaning "she is right in my eyes." This same idiom lies behind the Hebrew expression in 17:6 and 21:25, "Everyone did *what* was right in his own eyes." Samson's licentious behavior was simply a reflection of the undisciplined lifestyle of the age in which he lived.[5]

FAITH ALIVE

The eyes are the primary sense through which lustful temptation comes. That is why Job vowed, "I have made a covenant with my eyes; / Why then should I look upon a young woman?" (Job 31:1). Jesus in His teaching on adultery and lust advised, "If your right eyes causes you to sin, pluck it out and cast it from you" (Matt. 5:29). Blindness was preferable to spending eternity in hell. Jesus, of course, was not advising us to take His words to mutilate ourselves literally. He was using a figure of speech called hyperbole that uses exaggeration to capture our attention. Today the media bombards our eyes constantly, luring and enticing us with a variety of temptations.

How do you resist these ever-present visual temptations?

Do you have any rules in your home to regulate television and videos? What are they?

Have you, like Job, ever made a covenant with your eyes never to look lustfully on a member of the opposite sex? If not, why not make one now and ask for the Holy Spirit's enablement to keep it?

SAMSON'S VICTORY WITH A JAWBONE (JUDG. 15:1–20)

After the dust settles, Samson revisits his wife in Timnah. Because Samson seemingly abandoned her, the bride's father has now given her in marriage to Samson's best man. Again Samson becomes angry and in retaliation releases a blazing inferno into the Philistine fields—three hundred foxes tied end to end with a torch tucked between each pair of tails. When the Philistines learn the cause of the fire, they punish Samson by burning his bride and her father.

As the violence escalates, Samson revenges their deaths by slaughtering many Philistines. Samson flees to a cave in Judah for refuge. However, the Philistines threaten the tribe of Judah with invasion unless they hand over Samson. Samson allows himself to be taken by his countrymen, who hand him over to the Philistines tied up in two new ropes. As the Philistines attempt to kill their captive, the Spirit of the Lord comes mightily upon Samson. He easily breaks the ropes and, with the jawbone of a donkey, kills a thousand Philistines. After the slaughter Samson lies exhausted and thirsty, but God supernaturally provides water to revive him.

Who did Samson's father-in-law offer as a substitute bride? (Judg. 15:2)

To what are the ropes compared that fall from Samson's hands? (Judg. 15:14)

What was the name of the place where God split the hollow to bring forth water? (Judg. 15:19)

How many years was Samson a judge over Israel? (Judg. 15:20)

FAITH ALIVE

When Samson seeks revenge for his wife, the cycle of violence intensifies. In the destruction that follows, property is destroyed by fire and over a thousand are killed. Samson fails to heed the Lord's admonition spoken by Moses, "Vengeance is mine" (Deut. 32:35). Paul reiterates this principle in Romans 12:19 where he teaches forgiveness, not revenge.

Name a situation where you have wanted to get even with someone for what that person did to you.

How did you overcome your desire for revenge and instead forgive that individual?

Are there any people whom you still need to forgive? If so, list their names and how you intend to bring restoration to your relationship.

1.

2.

3.

SAMSON, DELILAH, AND FATAL VICTORY (JUDG. 16:1–31)

Samson's carnal appetites continue to get him into trouble. While Samson visits a harlot in Gaza, the city's residents lay a trap to kill him. At midnight Samson uses his supernatural strength to break out of the city, carrying the city's gates clear to Hebron. Then Samson falls in love with another Philistine woman named Delilah. Delilah's occupation is unknown, though she was perhaps a prostitute. She immediately becomes a pawn in the attempt of the Philistine rulers to kill Samson. Three times Delilah asks Samson for the secret of his strength, and three times he gives the wrong answer. The Philistines discover his lies when they try to capture him. Instead of learning his lesson, Samson falls for Delilah's line that, because he does not tell her his secret, he does not love her.

Finally, Samson breaks down and admits that his hair is the secret of his strength: as a Nazirite his hair has never been cut. That night Samson's locks are shorn, and with them his strength, although tragically he does not yet know that the Spirit has departed from him. When he awakens, he is at last a prisoner of the Philistines. They put out his eyes and make him a grinder in the prison at Gaza. On the day of a great sacrifice to the Philistine god Dagon, Samson is put on display in Dagon's temple as an object of mockery. Samson's hair has begun to grow back, and once last time he cries out to God for strength. He pushes aside the middle support pillars, causing the temple to collapse. Three thousand Philistine leaders are killed along with Samson. At his death Samson kills more Philistines than during his life.

What price did the Philistines offer Delilah for Samson's secret? (Judg. 16:5)

What three false answers did Samson give concerning how he could be weakened? (Judg. 16:7, 11, 13)

1.

2.

3.

How many locks of hair did Samson have on his head? (Judg. 16:19)

 FAITH ALIVE

Mike Fehlauer, the subject of our opening story, discovered seven steps that can be used to break bondage, sexual or otherwise.

1. Repent: This attacks the "victim" mentality.

2. Change your environment: This attacks the availability of sin.

3. Discover God's love: This attacks fear.

4. Develop godly relationships: This attacks deception.

5. Begin to think long term: This attacks lust.

6. Discover servanthood: This attacks pride.

7. Expect total deliverance: This attacks failure.[6]

Do you have an addiction that is ruling an area of your life? Identifying it is the first step toward freedom.

Have you told your spouse or close friend about your compulsion? Once the secret is out Satan loses his power.

Make a plan for recovery using the steps outlined by Pastor Mike Fehlauer.

 ## BIBLE EXTRA

Although the weaknesses of Samson and the other judges are clearly brought out in the Book of Judges, the writer of Hebrews remembers their positive contributions to Israel's deliverance. He includes four judges—Gideon, Barak, Samson, and Jephthah—in his list of ancient witnesses, "who through faith subdued kingdoms, worked righteousness, obtained promises" (Heb. 11:32–33). In spite of their failures, these judges were partakers of God's promises because of their faith. They are even today a part of that heavenly cloud who are encouraging us to endure and to fix our eyes on Jesus (Heb. 12:1–2).

FAITH ALIVE

Are you a person who only focuses on the shortcomings of people, or can you see their positive contributions in spite of weakness and failure?

How can you encourage people to live up to their potential in the kingdom of God?

1. Mike Fehlauer, "My Journey from Ministry to Sexual Addiction and Back" (*Ministries Today,* March/April 1995), 33–36.

2. *Nelson's New Illustrated Bible Dictionary* (Nashville: Thomas Nelson Publishers, 1995), 884, "Nazirite."

3. Ibid., 986–87, "Philistines."

4. *Word in Life Study Bible* (Nashville: Thomas Nelson Publishers, 1996), 459, map of "The Philistines."

5. *Spirit-Filled Life® Bible* (Nashville: Thomas Nelson Publishers, 1991), 370, note on Judges 14:3.

6. Mike Fehlauer, "My Journey from Ministry to Sexual Addiction and Back," 36, 38.

Lesson 12/Compromising God's Promise
Judges 17:1—21:25

"Wakantanka (Great Spirit), have mercy on us," the Sioux peyote leader sang as he closed the all-night prayer meeting in a tipi on a remote corner of the Pine Ridge Reservation.

Before our conversion to faith in Christ, my wife and I were members of a little-known religion called the Native American Church. This church legally uses the hallucinogenic cactus called peyote as its sacrament. The peyote cult began in the late 1800s under the leadership of a Comanche chief named Quanah Parker. Because of the spiritual void left by the destruction of their culture, the Plains Indians quickly embraced this new religious movement. Later the Sioux Indians modified the traditional liturgy by adding Christian elements. The use of tobacco during prayer was stopped, the half-moon altar was changed to the shape of a cross, a Bible was placed on the altar under the chief peyote fetish, and prayer was offered "in the name of Jesus."

Although raised in a mainline denomination, I had rejected Christianity and was searching spiritually in alternative religions such as the peyote cult. The unique blend of Christian symbols and Native American ritual seemed at first to meet my spiritual needs. Such syncretistic worship is not biblical, however, and the Holy Spirit had other plans for my wife and me. Friends saved out of the peyote cult began to witness to us. My mother and grandmother were praying for us, and an Indian pastor and his wife shared scriptural truth in Bible studies.

On Mother's Day, 1974, during a peyote meeting, both my wife and I separately committed our lives to Christ; we were spiritual twins born into the kingdom of God. We immediately left the Native American Church because our eyes were opened to its idolatrous worship. And we learned that God is jealous and does not tolerate His children serving other gods.

Similarly, idolatry and spiritual compromise were two major stumbling blocks that Israel confronted during her early history. The Book of Judges closes with two dramatic stories that illustrate the extent of Israel's spiritual and moral corruption.

MICAH LEADS DAN INTO IDOLATRY (JUDG. 17:1—18:31)

An Ephraimite named Micah confesses to his mother that he stole her eleven hundred shekels of silver. In gratitude for the money's return, she dedicates two hundred shekels to the Lord to make two images, despite a divine prohibition against such objects (Ex. 20:4–6). Micah now compromises the worship to the God of Israel by setting up a household shrine and consecrating his son as its priest, even though he is not a Levite. Later a Levite from Judah is traveling through Ephraim in hopes of finding a place to stay. Micah offers him the position of priest at his household shrine.

At that time, because Dan had failed to possess its inheritance, the tribe sends out five spies to look for other land to settle on. These Danites meet the Levite as they pass through Ephraim; and when he inquires of God for them, they receive His blessing for their journey. The spies locate an undefended city in the north and return to Zorah and Estaol with their recommendation to attack.

Six hundred armed Danites move out to capture Laish. On their way northward they pass the house of Micah in Ephraim. There they forcibly confiscate Micah's household shrine and offer the Levite the opportunity to be the priest of a tribe rather than of just one household. The Levite quickly forsakes his patron and joins the Danite army. When Micah discovers his gods and his priest missing, he leads an armed band to overtake the Danites. Faced with the superior Danite strength and their threat to kill him and his household, Micah backs down and returns to his house. The Danites continue northward, where they capture Laish and change its name to Dan. They create a shrine with the images stolen from Micah. The priest, a grand-son of Moses, and his sons serve at the Danite shrine until a later unspecified captivity.

What is the connection between the amount of money Micah stole and the sum paid Delilah to betray Samson? (Judg. 16:5; 17:2–3)

What items made up Micah's household shrine? (Judg. 17:5)

What motivated Micah to seek the services of the Levite? (Judg. 17:13)

What is the significance of the reference to the Danite camp at Mahaneh Dan? (Judg. 13:25; 18:12)

Who is the priest, and what is his family connection? (Judg. 18:30; Ex. 4:25; 1 Chr. 23:14–16)

BEHIND THE SCENES

What exactly were the idols used in the ancient world? The pagan nations around Israel worshiped a variety of idols, the most common being Baal and Asherah. Archaeological excavations have uncovered idols at sites throughout the Middle East. Because of Israel's close contact with her neigh-bors, it is natural that in times of spiritual decline, such as depicted in Judges, the people would begin to worship idols. Some Israelites, such as Micah, tried to blend the worship of God with the worship of idols, a process called syncretism. He was trying to make the invisible Almighty God more relevant and user-friendly by fashioning visible objects to be used in His worship. Thus at Micah's shrine there were three idolatrous objects—a carved image, a molded image, and an ephod. The carved image (Heb. *pesel*) is an object carved from wood or hewn from stone, which was occasionally overlaid with silver. The molded image (Heb. *massekah*) was poured or cast in a mold, either of silver or gold. The golden calves made by Aaron (Ex. 32:4) and Jereboam (1 Kin. 12:29) were fashioned in such a manner. Isaiah 40:19–20 vividly describes how such molded and carved images are made. The ephod was a linen garment, patterned after the outer vest worn by the high priest (Ex. 28:4–14; 39:2–7). The use of an ephod signified to observers that its wearer was performing a priestly service at the altar. In the New Testament period idols were also common throughout the Greco-Roman world. When Paul visited Athens, he was amazed at all the idols he saw in this supposedly intellectual center (Acts 17:16).[1]

Look up the following verses and state in your own words what they say to us as Christians regarding compromise with idols.

1 Corinthians 8:4; 10:14

Ephesians 5:5

Colossians 3:5

1 John 5:20

Revelation 22:14–15

FAITH ALIVE

What are the idols, if any, that are hindering your worship of God?

How do you intend to remove those idols from your life?

Have you made any spiritual compromises—Christian syncretism—in which, like Micah, you are trying to have both the world and the kingdom?

 ## BEHIND THE SCENES

The account of the Danite migration in Judges provides an important historical background for the settlement of the northernmost city in Israel. Sidonians apparently established the city of Laish in a lush valley along one of the sources of the Jordan River. Its isolation allowed the Danites to conquer it easily. They renamed the city Dan after their tribal name. Israel's territory was later said to encompass the north-south region extending from Dan to Beersheba (Judg. 20:1; 1 Sam. 3:20; etc.). Dan became famous as a center for apostate worship, given legitimacy by having Moses' descendants as its priests. It stood in opposition to the tabernacle at Shiloh, served by the high priest. When the kingdom divided in 931 B.C., Jeroboam established Dan and Bethel as religious centers to replace Jerusalem, which was in the southern kingdom. He made two golden calves and placed one in each city (1 Kin. 12:27–29). Idolatrous worship continued in Dan until the captivity under the Assyrian king Tiglath-Pileser in 733 B.C. (2 Kin. 15:29). The name Dan is synonymous with compromise in the Old Testament. Some scholars have suggested that this is perhaps the reason for its exclusion from the tribes of Israel listed in Revelation 7:5–8.[2]

THE SORDID TALE OF A CONCUBINE (JUDG. 19:1–30)

The second story also speaks of a Levite. Although there are several similarities between the Levites in these accounts, it is clear they are not the same person. Both live in the hills of

…ave family connections in Bethlehem of Judah, …omise their priestly calling.

…nt of the Levite and his concubine is a sordid … priest takes her as a concubine, the woman becomes a narlot and returns to her father's home in Bethlehem. The priest returns to Bethlehem to retrieve the woman, but it takes him five days to extricate himself from his father-in-law's hospitality. Once on the road the party of three, which includes a servant, turns aside from staying in the Jebusite city of Jebus (later Jerusalem) and instead decides to spend the night in the Israelite town of Gibeah. Although the travelers wait in the town square, no one invites them into their home. Finally, an old man who is an Ephraimite temporarily residing in Gibeah extends hospitality to the party, washing their feet and providing feed for their livestock.

That night a perverted crowd attempt to sexually assault the Levite guest. Instead the old man offers the deviants his virgin daughter and the concubine, but they persist in their demand for the man. Finally, the Levite throws his concubine to the men, who rape her repeatedly throughout the night. She staggers back to the doorstep, where the priest finds her dead in the morning. He takes his concubine's body back to Ephraim, and at his home cuts her corpse into twelve pieces and sends a part to each of the tribes of Israel.

The reaction to this deed is swift: there is a great outcry for action because nothing like this has ever happened in Israel's history. Centuries later Gibeah's horrible act was recalled by the prophet Hosea (Hos. 9:9; 10:9).

 FAITH ALIVE

Two significant problems of our day are highlighted in this story—sexual perversion and sexual abuse. As biblical values and morality diminish in Western society, promiscuity and pornography proliferate at an alarming rate. With the lowering of restraint, sexual aberrations are likewise increasing in society. The Corinthian Christians were saved out of a culture where homosexuality, fornication, and adultery were common. Yet through the power of Christ and the Holy Spirit, Paul writes, "And such were some of you" (1 Cor. 6:11). While we have all been tainted through contact with the debauchery around us, some have been saved especially from a lifestyle of sexual perversion and abuse. Using Paul's language from 1 Corinthians 6:11, describe how each of these divine actions has aided in your deliverance from bondage to sin.

Washed

Sanctified

Justified

BEHIND THE SCENES

The assault by the bisexual mob on the house in Gibeah is reminiscent of a similar assault on Lot's house in Sodom (Gen. 19:1–11). Both Lot and the old man offer their virgin daughters to the mob instead of their guests. Why would these fathers do such an awful thing to their own children?

The answer again lies in the nature of Middle Eastern hospitality. Once a guest is received into a household, it is the host's duty to serve and protect him. For Lot and the old Ephraimite to hand over their guests was to bring great disgrace upon them. Because the value of women was usually lower than a man in the ancient world, there was less shame in handing over their daughters.

Once again human custom has prevailed over the God-given command that parents should not prostitute their daughters (Lev. 19:29). As that Scripture warns, its outworking is that "the land become[s] full of wickedness"—Israel's precise situation during this period of Judges.

ISRAEL'S WAR WITH BENJAMIN (JUDG. 20:1–48)

The national outrage over the atrocity at Gibeah causes all Israel to assemble at Mizpah. After the Levite gives a firsthand account of his experience, the assembly draws lots to decide who should fight again the seven hundred men of Gibeah. When the tribe of Benjamin is asked to hand over the perpetrators of the crime, they refuse to turn in their brothers. The Benjamites now go to war against the rest of the tribes, badly outnumbered by a ratio of 15 to 1.

Once again Judah is chosen to lead the battle charge. The first two engagements bring large casualties to the Israelite army. The high priest Phinehas inquires of God at the ark of the covenant whether the battle should continue. God assures the Israelites that Gibeah will be conquered the next day. The initial defeat and subsequent victory through ambush after seeking the Lord closely resemble the situation at Ai (Josh. 7—8).

A holy war like that against the Canaanites is now directed against the tribe of Benjamin. The Israelites destroy men, women, and children as well as all the livestock. The destruction is so complete that only a remnant of soldiers from Benjamin remains.

How many Israelite soldiers assembled at Mizpah? (Judg. 20:2, 17)

How many soldiers of Benjamin were there? How many were from the town of Gibeah? (Judg. 20:15)

What did the Israelites do following their two defeats by the Benjamites? (Judg. 20:26–27)

How many Benjamites escaped and where did they flee? (Judg. 20:47)

FAITH ALIVE

Twice the Israelites attacked the Benjamites at the Lord's command, only to be defeated. On the third try the Benjamites are defeated. Why do you think the Israelites did not have an immediate victory on this occasion?

Name a time when God has led you to do something, but you did not have immediate success.

How did you respond to the situation and to God when you realized it was going to take repeated efforts for success? Did you persevere?

WIVES PROMISED FOR BENJAMIN'S SURVIVAL (JUDG. 21:1–25)

Before the Israelites go into battle, they swear that none of their daughters will marry a Benjamite. When the dust of battle settles, the people realize that one of their sister tribes is doomed to extinction. At a council they determine that the people of Jabesh Gilead failed to mobilize against the tribe of Benjamin. Ten thousand warriors go out against the city and destroy all its men, women, and children except four hundred virgins. These virgins are given as wives to the Benjamite survivors at the rock of Rimmon to perpetuate their tribe. However, they were still short two hundred virgins, so the Israelites devise another scheme to supply these additional brides. They advise the Benjamites to lie in wait at the yearly festival at Shiloh and to catch wives from the dancers who perform. Because the Israelite fathers have not given permission for this action, they are not guilty of breaking their oath. The Benjamites seize the needed wives and again reestablish their inheritance and rebuild their cities.

FAITH ALIVE

As if to justify the unusual behavior of the Israelites to secure wives for the Benjamites, the author of Judges closes the book with the familiar chorus, "In those days there was no king in Israel; everyone did what was right in his own eyes" (Judg. 21:25). In this chapter we see the difference between a good idea and a God idea, schemes born of the flesh and those born of the Spirit. Because of hasty decisions and unwarranted vows, the Israelites have put themselves into this dangerous predicament.

Name a situation where your good idea got you into trouble.

How did God help you get things straightened out?

What did you learn about moving forward with only God ideas?

BEHIND THE SCENES

The salvation of the tribe of Benjamin from extinction was certainly providential. Although it became the smallest of the tribes, Benjamin played an important role in Israel's later history. Saul, the first king of Israel, was from the tribe of Benjamin (1 Sam. 9:21) as was the second king, his son Ishbosheth (2 Sam. 2:8–10). Although the Benjamites were slow to recognize David as king, they eventually acclaimed him as their monarch (1 Chr. 12:29). When the nation divided into Israel and Judah under King Rehoboam (931 B.C.), the tribe of Benjamin was the only other tribe to align with Judah to form the southern kingdom (1 Kin. 12:21).

Other notables to arise from the tribe of Benjamin were

the prophet Jeremiah (Jer. 1:1) and Esther and her cousin Mordecai (Esth. 2:5). The most important Benjamite of the New Testament was the apostle Paul (Rom. 11:1). He proudly declared that he was "of the stock of Israel, of the tribe of Benjamin, a Hebrew of Hebrews" (Phil. 3:5). Benjamin's redemption therefore had important ramifications a thousand years later for the expansion of Christianity throughout the Roman Empire.

TRUTH-IN-ACTION THROUGH JUDGES[3]

The TRUTH-IN-ACTION through JUDGES
Letting the LIFE of the Holy Spirit Bring Faith's Works Alive in You!

Truth Judges Teaches	Text	**Action** Judges Invites
1 Guidelines for Growing in Godliness Judg. emphasizes the necessity of trusting God's presence and divine resources rather than our own. Even those talents and abilities we have from birth are corrupted by sin and must be energized by the Holy Spirit to bear fruit for God.	6:14, 16 10:13, 14	**Believe** that God strengthens those He calls and commissions. **Trust** in the promise of His abiding presence. **Heed God's warning: Do not** continue to **rely** upon your fleshly wisdom and ability lest God limit you to those resources rather than releasing His wisdom and power through you.
2 Keys to Wise Living Wisdom is knowing how to apply what you know to be true. Therefore, wisdom demands that you ascertain the Lord's direction and leadings for your life. Also, Judg. warns against assuming that all leadings are true. Self-righteousness and religious sentiment can be a source of serious deception.	6:36–40 17:3	**Test** and **confirm** any sense of divine leading. Refuse to move impulsively. **Be certain** of God's direction; it results in greater confidence. **Know that** God rejects any idolatry, regardless how religious or sincere one's sentiment may be. **Be wary** of religious deception.

The TRUTH-IN-ACTION through JUDGES
Letting the LIFE of the Holy Spirit Bring Faith's Works Alive in You!

Truth Judges Teaches	Text	Action Judges Invites
3 Steps to Dealing with Sin Sin presents a constant struggle with which we must deal or risk downfall. When we resist sin, we often feel the battle is over only to be tempted by the same sin again and again. Sin never goes away, and so we must constantly be on guard against it. However, even when we are overcome with sin, we have hope. God always gives another chance to turn from sin and back to Him.	2:2, 3 14:7 16:4–22 16:28	**Understand** that sins not dealt with radically and ruthlessly ultimately weaken and may cause downfall. **Persist** for victory in your struggle against sin. **Guard** against the seductions of the world and the flesh. **Understand** that compromise will eventually weaken and wear you out, giving the Evil One an occasion to overpower you. **Repent quickly** when overcome by sin. **Be confident** that God is faithful to honor all truly heartfelt repentance.
4 Lessons for Leaders Good leadership is a key to the triumph of God's purposes. Judg. underlines the need for godly leaders who speak with prophetic, anointed voices. When there is a lack of such leadership among God's people, the people lead unrestrained lives guided by their own opinions rather than God's Word and godly wisdom.	2:10–15 17:6; 18:1; 19:1; 21:25	**Know** that a lack of godly leadership will cause God's people to become worldly and incur God's judgment. **Strive** to become godly in your leadership. **Pursue** a prophetic dimension in your ministry.
5 Key Lessons in Faith Faith sees beyond trials and obstacles, knowing that God is sovereign over such and uses them to shape us and strengthen us for future battles. Faith also relies on an ever-present God to bring the necessary answer and supply the present need.	2:22; 3:2–4 4:9	**Accept** adversity and **welcome** opposition. **Believe** that God will use them to train you in obedience and strengthen you in spiritual warfare. **Avoid** relying upon men due to a lack of confidence in God's presence. Faith in God honors Him and results in your receiving what He intends for you.
6 Steps in Developing Humility Judg. stresses that humility is acknowledging that any good or righteous acts we accomplish result from God's working through us. We often think of humility as a weak self-abasement when, in fact, it is a bold confidence in a faithful God.	7:1–8 8:27	**Understand** that God's spiritual victory does not depend upon natural strength or ability. **Rely totally** upon God's enablement and strength. **Refuse** to build any monuments to your successes or victories. **Know** that they will likely become an occasion of stumbling for yourself and others.

1. *Nelson's New Illustrated Bible Dictionary* (Nashville: Thomas Nelson Publishers, 1995), 407–8, 590–92, "Ephod of High Priest," "Idol, Image," and "Idolatry."
2. Ibid., 324–25, "Dan," "Dan, Tribe of."
3. *Spirit-Filled Life® Bible* (Nashville: Thomas Nelson Publishers, 1991), 383–84, "Truth-in-Action through Judges."

SPIRIT-FILLED LIFE® BIBLE DISCOVERY GUIDE SERIES

B1   Genesis 0–8407–8515–1
B2   Exodus, Leviticus, Numbers, Deuteronomy
       0–8407–8513–5
B3   Joshua & Judges 0–7852–1242–6
B4   Ruth & Esther 0–7852–1130–0
B5   1 & 2 Samuel, 1 Chronicles 0–7852–1243–4
B6   1 & 2 Kings, 2 Chronicles   0–7852–1257–4
B7   Ezra & Nehemiah   0–7852–1258–2
B8*   Job, Ecclesiastes, Song of Songs
B9   Psalms 0–8407–8347–7
B10   Proverbs 0–7852–1167–5
B11   Isaiah 0–7852–1168–3
B12*   Jeremiah, Lamentations, Ezekiel
B13   Daniel & Revelation 0–8407–2081–5
B14   Hosea, Joel, Amos, Obadiah, Jonah, Micah, Nahum,
       Habakkuk, Zephaniah, Haggai, Zechariah, Malachi
       0–8407–2093–9
B15   Matthew, Mark, Luke 0–8407–2090–4
B16   John 0–8407–8349–3
B17   Acts 0–8407–8345–0
B18   Romans 0–8407–8350–7
B19   1 Corinthians 0–8407–8514–3
B20   2 Corinthians, 1 & 2 Timothy, Titus 0–7852–1204–3
B21   Galatians, 1 & 2 Thessalonians 0–7852–1134–9
B22   Ephesians, Philippians, Colossians, Philemon
       0–8407–8512–7
B23   Hebrews 0–8407–2082–3
B24   James, 1 & 2 Peter, 1–3 John, Jude 0–7852–1205–1
B25*   Getting to the Heart of the Bible (Key Themes:
       Basics of Bible Study)

*Coming Soon

SPIRIT-FILLED LIFE® KINGDOM DYNAMICS STUDY GUIDES

K1   People of the Spirit: Gifts, Fruit, and Fullness of the Holy Spirit   0–8407–8431–7

K2   Kingdom Warfare: Prayer, Spiritual Warfare, and the Ministry of Angels   0–8407–8433–3

K3   God's Way to Wholeness: Divine Healing by the Power of the Holy Spirit   0–8407–8430–9

K4   Life in the Kingdom: Foundations of the Faith   0–8407–8432–5

K5   Focusing on the Future: Key Prophecies and Practical Living   0–8407–8517–8

K6   Toward More Glorious Praise: Power Principles for Faith–Filled People   0–8407–8518–6

K7   Bible Ministries for Women: God's Daughters and God's Work   0–8407–8519–4

K8   People of the Covenant: God's New Covenant for Today   0–8407–8520–8

K9   Answering the Call to Evangelism: Spreading the Good News to Everyone   0–8407–2096–3

K10   Spirit-Filled Family: Holy Wisdom to Build Happy Homes   0–8407–2085–8

K11   Appointed to Leadership: God's Principles for Spiritual Leaders   0–8407–2083–1

K12   Power Faith: Balancing Faith in Words and Work   0–8407–2094–7

K13   Race & Reconciliation: Healing the Wounds, Winning the Harvest   0–7852–1131–4

K14   Praying in the Spirit: Heavenly Resources for Praise and Intercession   0–7852–1141–1

OTHER SPIRIT-FILLED LIFE® STUDY RESOURCES

Spirit-Filled Life® Bible, available in several bindings and in NKJV and KJV.

Spirit-Filled Life® Bible for Students

Hayford's Bible Handbook   0–8407–8359–0